教育部、国家语委重大文化工程
　　"中华思想文化术语传播工程"成果
国家社会科学基金重大项目
　　"中国核心术语国际影响力研究"（21&ZD158）
"十四五"国家重点出版物出版规划项目
获评第二届向全国推荐中华优秀传统文化普及图书

典藏版 · 第一卷

Key Concepts in Chinese Thought and Culture

中华思想文化术语 3

《中华思想文化术语》编委会 编

外语教学与研究出版社
FOREIGN LANGUAGE TEACHING AND RESEARCH PRESS
北京 BEIJING

图书在版编目（CIP）数据

中华思想文化术语：典藏版. 第一卷. 3：汉英对照 /《中华思想文化术语》编委会编. -- 北京：外语教学与研究出版社，2023.12
ISBN 978-7-5213-4878-1

Ⅰ. ①中… Ⅱ. ①中… Ⅲ. ①中华文化－术语－汉、英 Ⅳ. ①K203-61

中国国家版本馆 CIP 数据核字（2023）第 205210 号

出 版 人	王　芳
项目策划	刘旭璐
责任编辑	赵璞玉
责任校对	王海燕
封面设计	梧桐影
版式设计	孙莉明
出版发行	外语教学与研究出版社
社　　址	北京市西三环北路 19 号（100089）
网　　址	https://www.fltrp.com
印　　刷	三河市北燕印装有限公司
开　　本	710×1000　1/16
印　　张	57
版　　次	2024 年 1 月第 1 版　2024 年 1 月第 1 次印刷
书　　号	ISBN 978-7-5213-4878-1
定　　价	349.00 元（全五册）

如有图书采购需求，图书内容或印刷装订等问题，侵权、盗版书籍等线索，请拨打以下电话或关注官方服务号：
客服电话：400 898 7008
官方服务号：微信搜索并关注公众号"外研社官方服务号"
外研社购书网址：https://fltrp.tmall.com

物料号：348780001

"中华思想文化术语传播工程"专家团队
(按音序)

Scholars Participating in the Project "Key Concepts in Chinese Thought and Culture: Communication Through Translation"

顾问(Advisors)

李学勤(Li Xueqin)　　　林戊荪(Lin Wusun)
叶嘉莹(Florence Chia-ying Yeh)　　张岂之(Zhang Qizhi)
楼宇烈(Lou Yulie)　　　王　宁(Wang Ning)

专家委员会(Committee of Scholars)

主任(Director)

韩　震(Han Zhen)

委员(Members)

晁福林(Chao Fulin)　　　陈德彰(Chen Dezhang)
陈明明(Chen Mingming)　　冯志伟(Feng Zhiwei)
韩经太(Han Jingtai)　　　黄友义(Huang Youyi)
金元浦(Jin Yuanpu)　　　静　炜(Jing Wei)
李建中(Li Jianzhong)　　李雪涛(Li Xuetao)
李照国(Li Zhaoguo)　　　聂长顺(Nie Changshun)
潘公凯(Pan Gongkai)　　　王　博(Wang Bo)

王柯平（Wang Keping） 叶　朗（Ye Lang）
袁济喜（Yuan Jixi） 袁行霈（Yuan Xingpei）
张　晶（Zhang Jing） 张立文（Zhang Liwen）
张西平（Zhang Xiping） 郑述谱（Zheng Shupu）

特邀汉学家（Scholars of China Studies）

艾　恺（Guy Salvatore Alitto） 安乐哲（Roger T. Ames）
白罗米（Luminița Bălan） 包华石（Martin Joseph Powers）
陈瑞河（Madaras Réka） 狄伯杰（B. R. Deepak）
顾　彬（Wolfgang Kubin） 韩安德（Harry Anders Hansson）
韩　裴（Petko Todorov Hinov） 柯鸿冈（Paul Crook）
柯马凯（Michael Crook） 斯巴修（Iljaz Spahiu）
王健、李盈（Jan & Yvonne Walls） 魏查理（Charles Willemen）

学术委员会（Academic Committee）

白振奎（Bai Zhenkui） 蔡力坚（Cai Lijian）
曹轩梓（Cao Xuanzi） 陈海燕（Chen Haiyan）
陈少明（Chen Shaoming） 程景牧（Cheng Jingmu）
丁　浩（Ding Hao） 付志斌（Fu Zhibin）
干春松（Gan Chunsong） 郭晓东（Guo Xiaodong）
韩志华（Han Zhihua） 何　淼（He Miao）
何世剑（He Shijian） 胡　海（Hu Hai）
贾德忠（Jia Dezhong） 姜海龙（Jiang Hailong）
柯修文（Daniel Canaris） 黎　臻（Li Zhen）

李存山（Li Cunshan）	李恭忠（Li Gongzhong）
李景林（Li Jinglin）	林敏洁（Lin Minjie）
林少阳（Lin Shaoyang）	刘　佳（Liu Jia）
刘　璐（Liu Lu）	刘　青（Liu Qing）
吕玉华（Lü Yuhua）	梅缵月（Mei Zuanyue）
孟庆楠（Meng Qingnan）	裴德思（Thorsten Pattberg）
彭冬林（Peng Donglin）	乔　希（Joshua Mason）
任大援（Ren Dayuan）	邵亦鹏（Shao Yipeng）
沈卫星（Shen Weixing）	施晓菁（Lynette Shi）
陶黎庆（Tao Liqing）	童孝华（Tong Xiaohua）
王丽丽（Wang Lili）	王　琳（Wang Lin）
王明杰（Wang Mingjie）	王维东（Wang Weidong）
王　鑫（Wang Xin）	温海明（Wen Haiming）
吴根友（Wu Genyou）	吴礼敬（Wu Lijing）
夏　晶（Xia Jing）	谢远笋（Xie Yuansun）
辛红娟（Xin Hongjuan）	徐明强（Xu Mingqiang）
徐亚男（Xu Yanan）	许家星（Xu Jiaxing）
严学军（Yan Xuejun）	张　静（Zhang Jing）
张子尧（Zhang Ziyao）	章思英（Zhang Siying）
章伟文（Zhang Weiwen）	赵　桐（Zhao Tong）
赵　悠（Zhao You）	郑　开（Zheng Kai）
周云帆（Zhou Yunfan）	朱绩崧（Zhu Jisong）
朱良志（Zhu Liangzhi）	朱　渊（Zhu Yuan）
左　励（Zuo Li）	

前言

"中华思想文化术语"的定义可以表述为：由中华民族所创造或构建，凝聚、浓缩了中华哲学思想、人文精神、思维方式、价值观念，以词或短语形式固化的概念和文化核心词。它们是中华民族几千年来对自然与社会进行探索和理性思索的成果，积淀着中华民族的历史智慧，反映中华民族最深沉的精神追求以及理性思索的深度与广度；其所蕴含的人文思想、思维方式、价值观念已经作为一种"生命基因"深深融于中华子孙的血液，内化为中华民族共同的性格和信仰，并由此支撑起中华数千年的学术传统、思想文化和精神世界。它是当代中国人理解中国古代哲学思想、人文精神、思维方式、价值观念之变化乃至文学艺术、历史等各领域发展的核心关键，也是世界其他国家和民族了解当代中国、中华民族和海外华人之精神世界的钥匙。

当今世界已进入文化多元与话语多极时代。世界不同区域、不同国家、不同民族的文明，其流动融合之快、之广、之深超过历史任何时期。每个国家和民族都有自己独具的思想文化和话语体系，都应在世界文明、世界话语体系中占有一席之地，得到它应有的地位和尊重。而思想文化术语无疑是一个国家和民族话语体系中最核心、最本质的部分，是它的思想之"髓"、文化之"根"、精神之"魂"、学术之"核"。越来越多的有识之士认识到，中华思想文化蕴藏着解决当今人类所面临的许多难题的重要启示，中华民族所倡导的"厚德载物""道法自然""天人合一""和而不同""民惟邦本""经世致用"等思想，以及它所追求的"协和万邦""天下一家"、世界"大同"，代表了当今世界文明的发展趋势，也因此成为国际社会的共识。越来越多的外国学者和友人对中华思想文化及其术语产生浓厚的兴趣，希望有更全面、更进一步的了解。

今天我们整理、诠释、翻译、传播中华思想文化术语，目的是立足于中华思想文化，通过全面系统的整理与诠释，深度挖掘其中既能反映中华哲学思想、人文精神、思维方式、价值观念、文化特征，又具跨越时空、超越国度之意义，以及富有永恒魅力与当代价值的含义和内容，并将其译成英语等语言，让世界更客观、更全面地认识中国，了解中华民族的过去和现在，了解当代中国人及海外华人的精神世界，从而推动国家间的平等对话及不同文明间的交流借鉴。

中华思想文化术语的整理、诠释和英语翻译得到了中国教育部、中国国际出版集团、中央编译局、北京大学、中国人民大学、武汉大学、北京外国语大学等单位的大力支持，得到了叶嘉莹、李学勤、张岂之、林戊荪、楼宇烈、王宁等海内外众多知名学者的支持。需要说明的是，"中华思想文化术语"这个概念是首次提出，其内涵和外延还有待学界更深入的研究；而且，如此大规模地整理、诠释、翻译中华思想文化术语，在中国也是首次，无成例可循。因此，我们的诠释与翻译一定还有待完善的地方，我们会及时吸纳广大读者的意见，不断提高术语诠释与翻译的质量。

2021 年 12 月 11 日

Foreword

By "key concepts in Chinese thought and culture" we mean concepts and keywords or phrases the Chinese people have created or come to use and that are fundamentally pertinent to Chinese philosophy, humanistic spirit, way of thinking, and values. They represent the Chinese people's exploration of and rational thinking about nature and society over thousands of years. These concepts and expressions reflect the Chinese people's wisdom, their profound spiritual pursuit, as well as the depth and width of their thinking. Their way of thinking, values, and philosophy embodied in these concepts have become a kind of "life gene" in Chinese culture, and have long crystallized into the common personality and beliefs of the Chinese nation. For the Chinese people today, they serve as a key to a better understanding of the evolutions of their ancient philosophy, humanistic spirit, way of thinking, and values as well as the development of Chinese literature, art, and history. For people in other countries, these concepts open the door to understanding the spiritual world of contemporary China and the Chinese people, including those living overseas.

In the era of cultural diversity and multipolar discourse today, cultures of different countries and civilizations of different peoples are integrating faster, in greater depth, and on a greater scope than ever before. All countries and peoples have their own systems of thought, culture, and discourse, which should all have their place in the civilization and discourse systems of the world. They all deserve due respect. The concepts in thought and culture of a country and its people are naturally the most essential part of their discourse. They constitute the marrow of a nation's thought, the root of its culture, the soul of its spirit, and the core of its scholarship. More and more people of vision have come to recognize the inspirations Chinese thought and culture might offer to help resolve many difficult problems faced by mankind. The Chinese hold that a man should "have ample virtue and carry all things," "Dao operates naturally," "heaven and man are united as one," a man of virtue seeks "harmony but not uniformity," "people are the foundation of the state," and "study of ancient classics should meet present needs." The Chinese ideals such as "coexistence of all in harmony," "all the people under heaven are one family," and a world of "universal harmony" are drawing increasing attention among the international community. More and more international scholars and friends have become interested in learning and better understanding Chinese thought and culture in general, and the relevant concepts in particular.

In selecting, explaining, translating, and sharing concepts in Chinese thought and culture, we have adopted a comprehensive and systematic approach. Most of them not only reflect the characteristics of Chinese philosophy, humanistic spirit, way of thinking, values, and culture, but also have significance and/or implications that transcend time and national boundaries, and that still fascinate present-day readers and offer them food for thought. It is hoped that the translation of these concepts into English and other languages will help people in other countries to gain a more objective and more rounded understanding of China, of its people, of its past and present, and of the spiritual world of contemporary Chinese. Such understanding should be conducive to promoting equal dialogue between China and other countries and exchanges between different civilizations.

The selection, explanation, and translation of these concepts have been made possible thanks to the support of the Ministry of Education, China International Publishing Group, the Central Compilation and Translation Bureau, Peking University, Renmin University of China, Wuhan University, and Beijing Foreign Studies University, as well as the support of renowned scholars in China and abroad, including Florence Chia-ying Yeh, Li Xueqin, Zhang Qizhi, Lin Wusun, Lou Yulie, and Wang Ning.

The idea of compiling key concepts in Chinese thought and culture represents an innovation and the project calls much research and effort both in connotation and denotation. Furthermore, an endeavor like this has not been previously attempted on such a large scale. Lack of precedents means there must remain much room for improvement. Therefore, we welcome comments from all readers in the hope of better fulfilling this task.

December 11, 2021

目录
Contents

1. báimiáo 白描
   Plain Line Drawing 1

2. biànhuà 变化
   Change 3

3. chényù 沉郁
   Melancholy 4

4. chéngyì 诚意
   Be Sincere in Thought 5

5. 《Chūnqiū》、Chūnqiū 春秋
   The Spring and Autumn Annals / The Spring and Autumn Period 7

6. cí 词
   Ci (Lyric) 9

7. cíqǔ 词曲
   Ci (Lyric) and *Qu* (Melody) 11

8. cuòcǎi-lòujīn 错彩镂金
   Gilded and Colored 12

9. dàdào-zhìjiǎn 大道至简
   Great Truth in Simple Words 13

10. dàqiǎo-ruòzhuō 大巧若拙
    Exquisite Skill Looks Simple and Clumsy 15

11. dàtǐ / xiǎotǐ 大体 / 小体
    The Major Organ and the Minor Organs 17

12 *dàyòng* 大用
Maximal Functioning 18

13 *dānqīng* 丹青
Painting in Colors 19

14 *dànbó* 淡泊
Quiet Living with No Worldly Desire 21

15 *dànbó-míngzhì, níngjìng-zhìyuǎn* 淡泊明志，宁静致远
Indifference to Fame and Fortune Characterizes a High Aim in Life, and Leading a Quiet Life Helps One Accomplish Something Lasting ... 22

16 *dāngháng* 当行
Professionalism 23

17 *dàojìtiānxià* 道济天下
Support All People by Upholding Truth and Justice 25

18 *dédào-duōzhù, shīdào-guǎzhù* 得道多助，失道寡助
A Just Cause Enjoys Abundant Support While an Unjust Cause Finds Little 27

19 *déxìngzhīzhī* 德性之知
Knowledge from One's Moral Nature 29

20 *diǎnyǎ* 典雅
Classical Elegance 30

21 *dǐng* 鼎
Ding (Vessel) 32

22	dòngjìng 动静	
	Movement and Stillness	33
23	duō xíng bù yì bì zì bì 多行不义必自毙	
	He Who Repeatedly Commits Wrongdoing Will Come to No Good End.	34
24	fánrù 繁缛	
	Overly Elaborative	35
25	fēnggǔ 风骨	
	Fenggu	37
26	fēngjiào 风教	
	Moral Cultivation	39
27	fúróng-chūshuǐ 芙蓉出水	
	Lotus Rising Out of Water	41
28	gāngróu-xiāngjì 刚柔相济	
	Combine Toughness with Softness	43
29	gē 歌	
	Song	44
30	gégù-dǐngxīn 革故鼎新	
	Do Away with the Old and Set Up the New	45
31	gōng shēng míng, lián shēng wēi 公生明，廉生威	
	Fairness Fosters Discernment and Integrity Creates Authority.	47

32 hàoránzhīqì 浩然之气
Noble Spirit 48

33 jìtuō 寄托
Entrust One's Thoughts and Feelings to Imagery 49

34 jiànlì-sīyì 见利思义
Think of Righteousness in the Face of Gain 51

35 jiànwénzhīzhī 见闻之知
Knowledge from One's Senses 52

36 jiànxián-sīqí 见贤思齐
When Seeing a Person of High Caliber, Strive to Be His Equal 53

37 jiàngǔ-zhījīn 鉴古知今
Review the Past to Understand the Present 54

38 jìnxīn 尽心
Exert One's Heart / Mind to the Utmost 56

39 kōnglíng 空灵
Ethereal Effect 57

40 kuàngdá 旷达
Broad-mindedness / Unconstrained Style 59

41 lǐshàngwǎnglái 礼尚往来
Reciprocity as a Social Norm 61

42 lǐyī-fēnshū 理一分殊
There Is But One *Li* (Universal Principle), Which Exists in
Diverse Forms. 62

43 nèiměi 内美
Inner Beauty 64

44 pǐjí-tàilái 否极泰来
When Worse Comes to the Worst, Things Will Turn for the Better. 65

45 piāoyì 飘逸
Natural Grace. 67

46 qíwù 齐物
See Things as Equal. 68

47 qìgǔ 气骨
Qigu (Emotional Vitality and Forcefulness) 69

48 qìzhìzhīxìng 气质之性
Character Endowed by *Qi* (Vital Force) 70

49 qì 器
Qi (Vessel) 72

50 qiánshì-bùwàng, hòushìzhīshī 前事不忘，后事之师
Past Experience, If Not Forgotten, Is a Guide for the Future. 73

51 qiú fàngxīn 求放心
Search for the Lost Heart. 75

15

52 qǔ 曲
   Qu (Melody) 76

53 rénzhě-àirén 仁者爱人
   A Benevolent Person Loves Others. 78

54 sānbiǎo 三表
   Three Standards 79

55 sāncái 三才
   Three Elements 80

56 sānsī'érxíng 三思而行
   Think Carefully Before Taking Action 82

57 shèndú 慎独
   Shendu (Ethical Self-cultivation) 83

58 shènsī-míngbiàn 慎思明辨
   Careful Reflection and Clear Discrimination 85

59 shīzhí-wéizhuàng 师直为壮
   Troops Will Be Powerful When Fighting a Just Cause. 86

60 shī 诗
   Shi (Poetry) 87

61 shòurényǐyú 授人以渔
   Teaching How to Fish 90

62 shù 恕
   Being Considerate / Forgiveness 91

63 sìhǎi zhī nèi jiē xiōngdì 四海之内皆兄弟
All the People Within the Four Seas Are Brothers. 92

64 tàixū 太虚
Taixu (Great Void) 93

65 tiāndào 天道
Way of Heaven 94

66 tiānlǐ 天理
Natural Law / Principles of Heaven 96

67 tiānmìng 天命
Mandate of Heaven 97

68 tiānmìngzhīxìng 天命之性
Character Endowed by Heaven 98

69 tiānxià-xīngwáng, pǐfū-yǒuzé 天下兴亡，匹夫有责
Survival of a Nation Is the Responsibility of Every Individual. 100

70 tóngguī-shūtú 同归殊途
Arrive at the Same Destination via Different Routes / Rely on a
Common Ontological Entity 102

71 wēngù-zhīxīn 温故知新
Review the Old and Learn the New 104

72 wúyù-zégāng 无欲则刚
People with No Covetous Desires Stand Upright. 105

73 xiāngfǎn-xiāngchéng 相反相成
Being both Opposite and Complementary 107

74 xiàng 象
Xiang (Semblance) 108

75 xiǎoshuō 小说
Fiction 110

76 xiěyì 写意
Freehand Brushwork 112

77 xīnzhī 心知
Mind Cognition 114

78 xíngxiān-zhīhòu 行先知后
First Action, Then Knowledge 116

79 xuán 玄
Xuan (Mystery) 117

80 xuèqì 血气
Vitality / Vital Force 118

81 xúnmíng-zéshí 循名责实
Hold Actualities According to Its Name 119

82 yǎyuè 雅乐
Fine Music 121

83 yánbùjìnyì 言不尽意
Words Cannot Fully Express Thought 123

84 yánjìnyì 言尽意
Words Can Fully Express Thought. 124

85 Yán-Huáng 炎黄
The Fiery Emperor and the Yellow Emperor / Emperor Yan and
Emperor Huang.. 126

86 yīwù-liǎngtǐ 一物两体
One Thing in Two Fundamental States... 128

87 yǐ wú wéi běn 以无为本
Wu Is the Origin. 129

88 yǐzhí-bàoyuàn 以直报怨
Repay a Grudge with Rectitude 130

89 yǒuróng-nǎidà 有容乃大
A Broad Mind Achieves Greatness... 131

90 yǔmín-gēngshǐ 与民更始
Make a Fresh Start with the People 133

91 zàizhōu-fùzhōu 载舟覆舟
Carry or Overturn the Boat / Make or Break 134

92 zhèngmíng 正名
Rectification of Names... 135

93 zhèngxīn 正心
Rectify One's Heart / Mind 136

19

94 zhèngzhě-zhèngyě 政者正也
Governance Means Rectitude. 138

95 zhī chǐ ér hòu yǒng 知耻而后勇
Having a Feeling of Shame Gives Rise to Courage. 139

96 zhīxíng-héyī 知行合一
Unity of Knowledge and Action 140

97 zhīxiān-xínghòu 知先行后
First Knowledge, Then Action 142

98 zhí 直
Rectitude 144

99 zhì dà guó ruò pēng xiǎo xiān 治大国若烹小鲜
Governing a Big Country Is Like Cooking Small Fish. 145

100 zhōng 忠
Loyalty 147

术语表 List of Concepts 148
中国历史年代简表 A Brief Chronology of Chinese History 153

báimiáo 白描

Plain Line Drawing

中国画的表现手法之一。用墨线勾勒描摹物象的轮廓，不设颜色。白描多用于画人物、花卉，着墨不多，气韵生动。白描源于古代的"白画"。一般运用同一墨色，通过线条的长短、粗细、轻重、转折等表现物象的质感和动势。白描流行于晋唐时期，宋代以后自成一格。晋代顾恺之（345？—409）、北宋李公麟（1049—1106）、元代赵孟𫖯（1254—1322）等擅长铁线描，唐代吴道子、南宋马和之等擅长兰叶描。白描也是文学创作中非常重要的表现手法，主要指用朴素简练的笔墨，不加烘托渲染，描绘出鲜明生动的形象。古典小说《水浒传》《三国演义》等多有高超的白描手法。

Plain line drawing is one of the traditional Chinese styles of artistic presentation. It features the contours of images sketched in black ink lines. This style of painting is mostly used in painting human figures and flowers. Although not much ink is applied, this technique can achieve a very lively effect. Plain line drawing originated from the plain drawing of earlier times; through variations in lines' length, thickness, pressure, and changes in trajectory, the artist can portray the texture and motion of images. Plain line drawing was prevalent from the Jin Dynasty through the Tang Dynasty. During the Song Dynasty, it formed a distinctive style of its own. Gu Kaizhi (345?-409) of the Jin Dynasty, Li Gonglin (1049-1106) of the Northern Song Dynasty, and Zhao Mengfu (1254-1322) of the Yuan Dynasty specialized in painting lines of perfectly even width like iron wire, while Wu Daozi of the Tang Dynasty and Ma Hezhi of the Southern Song Dynasty were renowned for their skill in drawing thick, wavy lines resembling orchid leaves. Plain drawing is also a very important style of expression in narrative literature. In this context it refers to a simple and concise style of writing, without embellishment, so as to produce fresh, lively images. In classic novels such as *Outlaws of the Marsh* or *Romance of the Three Kingdoms*, one finds abundant instances of a plain drawing style of writing.

引例 Citation：

◎白描画易纤弱柔媚，最难遒劲高逸，今观此图如屈铁丝，唐有阎令，宋有伯时，元有赵文敏，可称鼎足矣。（王穉登《题李龙眠〈维摩演教图〉》）
（白描所描摹出的画作容易流于纤细瘦弱、阴柔妩媚，最难表现遒劲有力、高古飘逸的感觉，而今观赏此画，用笔好似弯曲铁丝一般［刚劲有力］，唐代的阎立本、北宋的李公麟、元代的赵孟頫可称得上三足鼎立。）

Paintings drawn with plain lines are prone to being overly fine or weak, often lacking a soaring spirit and vigor despite a feminine beauty. But today, after admiring this particular painting, I have found its strokes to be vigorous like bent wire. (When it comes to vigorous brushwork,) Yan Liben of the Tang Dynasty, Li Gonglin of the Northern Song Dynasty, and Zhao Mengfu of the Yuan Dynasty were three eminent figures. (Wang Zhideng: Postscript to Li Longmian's "Korimaro Preaches a Sermon")

biànhuà 变化

Change

事物存在的基本状态。"变"与"化"既可合而言之，也可以分别而论。在区别的意义上，"变"指显著的变化，"化"指隐微、逐渐的变化。一般认为，天地万物包括人与社会，都处于"变化"之中。只有不断"变化"，才能长久地存在和发展。"变化"的原因在于人和事物所具有的对立属性之间不断碰撞、交合。有人认为"变化"遵循着恒常的法则，是可以认识和把握的；但也有人主张"变化"是无常的，难以把握。而佛教则认为万物的"变化"都是虚假的，万物是寂静不迁的。

The term refers to the fundamental state of the existence of things. *Bian* (变) and *hua* (化) may be used as one word or separately. Specifically, *bian* means manifest change, while *hua* indicates subtle and gradual change. Ancient Chinese thinkers generally held that all things under heaven and on earth, including humans and society, are all in a state of change. Only through constant change can they permanently exist and develop. Change is caused by constant clash and integration between the conflicting properties with which people and things are endowed. Some scholars believed that change follows a constant law and can thus be understood and grasped, while others maintained that change is unpredictable and therefore difficult to grasp. Buddhism, on the other hand, holds that changes of things are only superficial, and that all things are still and motionless.

引例 Citations：

◎刚柔相推而生变化。(《周易·系辞上》)

（刚与柔之间相互推移而产生变化。）

The interaction between firmness and gentleness produces change. (*The Book of Changes*)

◎变言其著，化言其渐。（张载《横渠易说·乾》）

（"变"说的是事物显著的变化，"化"说的是事物隐微逐渐的变化。）

Bian refers to obvious changes of things, while *hua* suggests gradual changes of things. (Zhang Zai: *Zhang Zai's Explanation of The Book of Changes*)

chényù 沉郁

Melancholy

指诗歌作品中所表现出的情志含蓄深沉、意蕴丰富深厚的艺术风格。以杜甫（712—770）为代表的古代诗人，关注国家大事，忧心民生艰难，苦思国家兴衰存亡之理而难通，求索安邦济民之策而不得，反映在作品中就表现为情志含蓄深沉、思想丰富深厚。其作品常常一唱三叹，结构、节奏、音调等抑扬起伏，给予读者以特有的"顿挫"美感，读后产生回味无穷的感受。

Melancholy refers to an artistic style in poetic works in which sentiment expressed is subtle and the message is profound. Ancient Chinese poets represented by Du Fu (712-770), keenly concerned about state affairs and people's hardships, tried hard to understand what caused the rise and fall of a nation and sought ways to save the country and the people, but all to no avail. Such frustration and disappointment are thus reflected in their poems. With meticulously crafted structure, rhythm, and tones, their works give readers a special aesthetic appreciation of melody and infinite afterthought.

引例 Citation：

◎所谓沈（chén）郁者，意在笔先，神余言外。（陈廷焯《白雨斋词话》卷一）
（所谓"沉郁"，是指动笔前已有长时间的思想感情积蓄，因而文章有着语言所不能穷尽的精神蕴含。）

Melancholy means that as a writer has given so much thought to the theme before writing, his work, once completed, contains profound sentiments beyond description. (Chen Tingzhuo: *Remarks on Ci Poetry from White Rain Studio*)

chéngyì 诚意

Be Sincere in Thought

使追求日用伦常之道的意愿真实无妄。"诚意"出自《大学》，与格物、致知、正心、修身、齐家、治国、平天下并称"八条目"，是儒家所倡导的道德修养的一个重要环节。"诚意"以"致知"为前提。在知晓日用伦常之道的基础上，确立起内心对此道的认同与追求。内心的真实意愿会自然地表现于言行之中。个人的道德行为应出于真实的意愿，而不应在没有真实意愿的情况下仅仅使外在的言行符合道德规范。

The pursuit of moral principles in daily life should be true and sincere. "Being sincere in thought" is one of the "eight essential principles" from the philosophical text *The Great Learning*, the other seven being "studying things," "acquiring knowledge," "rectifying one's mind," "cultivating oneself," "regulating one's family well," "governing the state properly," and "bringing peace to all under heaven." Those constitute important stages in the moral cultivation advocated by Confucian scholars. "Sincerity in thought" has as its preceding stage the "extension of knowledge." One can only identify and follow the principle of "sincerity in thought" on the basis of understanding the moral principles in daily life. One's true desire will then naturally reflect itself in one's daily behavior. An individual's moral conduct must stem from a genuine wish and must not just conform superficially to the moral principles without true intention of practicing them.

引例 Citations：

◎所谓诚其意者，毋自欺也。如恶恶臭，如好好色，此之谓自谦（qiè）。（《礼记·大学》）

（所谓诚意，就是不要自己欺骗自己。如同厌恶难闻的味道，如同喜爱美色，这叫做自我满足。）

Being sincere in one's thought is to tolerate no self-deception, as one hates undesirable smells or likes lovely colors. That is what is called satisfied with oneself. (*The Book of Rites*)

◎诚其意者，自修之首也。（朱熹《大学章句》）

（"诚意"是个人自我修养的首要任务。）

Being sincere in thought is of primary importance in self-cultivation. (Zhu Xi: *Annotations on The Great Learning*)

《Chūnqiū》, Chūnqiū 春秋

The Spring and Autumn Annals / The Spring and Autumn Period

儒家经典之一。相传由孔子（前551—前479）根据鲁国编年史编订加工而成，记载了鲁隐公元年（前722）至鲁哀公十四年（前481）间计242年的历史。《春秋》是编年体史书的始祖，故而亦作为编年体史书的通称。《春秋》纪事简短，文字凝练，后世儒者认为它含有"微言大义"，将这种委婉曲折而寓褒贬的写作手法称为"春秋笔法"。解释《春秋》的有《左传》《公羊传》《穀梁传》，合称"《春秋》三传"（其中，《公羊传》和《穀梁传》主要解释《春秋》义理，而《左传》记载这一时期的史实，与解经没有关系）。"春秋"也用来指"春秋时代"（因《春秋》得名），其起讫年代，有两种说法：一指《春秋》所记载的历史时期，一指自公元前770年周平王东迁至前476年这一时期。

The Spring and Autumn Annals is one of the Confucian classics, believed to have been compiled by Confucius (551-479 BC) based on the chronicles of the State of Lu. The book covers a period of 242 years from the first year of the reign of Duke Yin of Lu (722 BC) to the 14th year of the reign of Duke Ai (481 BC). The book was China's first chronological history, and its title has come to mean all chronological histories. Its records of events are brief and its style is concise. Later Confucian scholars regarded the book as having "subtle words with profound meanings," and described its implied and indirect style of writing, which makes both positive and negative criticism, as "the style of *The Spring and Autumn Annals*." *Zuo's Commentary on The Spring and Autumn Annals*, *Gongyang's Commentary on The Spring and Autumn Annals*, and *Guliang's*

Commentary on The Spring and Autumn Annals, together known as the "Three Commentaries," are explications of this work. (Gongyang's and Guliang's commentaries explain the reasoning in the book, while Zuo's commentary records historical events of this period but does not interpret The Spring and Autumn Annals.) "Spring and Autumn" also refers to the Spring and Autumn Period, an era named after The Spring and Autumn Annals. There are two views about the period it spans. One is the period covered in the Annals; the other is the period from 770 BC, when King Ping of Zhou moved his capital from near present-day Xi'an in the west to present-day Luoyang in the east, until the year of 476 BC.

引例 Citations：

◎故君子曰："《春秋》之称微而显，志而晦，婉而成章，尽而不污，惩恶而劝善，非圣人谁能修之？"(《左传·成公十四年》)
(所以君子说："《春秋》用词细微而意义显豁，记述史实而内容幽深，婉转有致但顺理成章，直言其事绝不迂曲，惩戒邪恶而勉励向善。如果不是圣人，谁能够编写？")

Therefore the noble man said, "The style of The Spring and Autumn Annals is implicit but the meaning of the book is clear; it records both events and their profound significance. It is subtle yet logical, thorough yet not verbose. It chastises evil deeds and urges people to do good deeds. Who but a sage could have compiled this?" (Zuo's Commentary on The Spring and Autumn Annals)

◎世衰道微，邪说暴行有作，臣弑其君者有之，子弑其父者有之。孔子惧，作《春秋》。(《孟子·滕文公下》)
(世风道德逐渐衰微，荒谬学说和残暴行径不断出现，有臣子杀死君王的，有儿子杀死父亲的。孔子深为忧虑，所以编写了《春秋》。)

Social mores and moral conduct were in decline; evil theories and violent deeds kept emerging; some subjects killed their rulers and some sons killed their fathers. Deeply worried, Confucius compiled *The Spring and Autumn Annals*. (*Mencius*)

cí 词

Ci (Lyric)

起源于唐五代、发展成熟于宋代的一种新的文学体式，也称"曲子词""乐府""长短句"等。由诗发展演变而来，其主要特点是配乐歌唱。每首词都有一个调名，称"词牌"。不同的词牌在句数及每句的字数、平仄、押韵上都有严格的规定。从篇幅看，词可分为小令、中调、长调；从音乐体制看，词一般分上下两段（古人称为"阕"或"片"），也有分成三四段或仅有一段的，因之音乐也有演奏一遍和多遍的区别；从风格看，词基本分为婉约和豪放两大派：婉约派风格婉转含蓄，多写儿女情长；豪放派则摄取人生情怀及家国大事入词，境界宏大。宋代许多文人学者喜好填词作曲，对推动词的发展起了重要作用。后世的词一般不再配乐歌唱，基本成为按谱填词的一种文学形式。

Ci (词) originated in the Tang and the Five Dynasties, and developed to maturity as a new literary form in the Song Dynasty. Also known as "lyric with a melody," "*yuefu* (乐府) poetry" or "long and short verses," *ci* developed from poetry. Its main feature is that it is set to music and sung. Each piece of *ci* has a name for its tune. There are strict requirements for the number of lines and the number of characters as well as tone pattern and rhyming in different tunes. In terms of length, *ci* is divided into short lyrics, medium lyrics, and long lyrics. In terms of musical system, a piece of *ci* is usually divided into two stanzas of *que* (阕) or *pian* (片), as ancient Chinese called them. Occasionally, it consists of three or four stanzas, or just one. Thus, the music can be played once or many times. In terms of style, *ci* falls into the graceful and restrained school and the bold and unconstrained school. The former is delicate and sentimental, often describing family life and love, while the latter is bold and free, often expressing one's vision about major social issues like the fate of the nation. Many literati and scholars of the Song Dynasty composed *ci* lyrics, which played a significant part in promoting its development. Today, *ci* is generally not set to music and sung. Rather, it is a literary form composed in accordance with the requirements of a music tune.

引例 Citations：

◎古乐府有曰"辞"者，有曰"曲"者，其实"辞"即曲之辞，"曲"即辞之曲也。（刘熙载《艺概·词曲概》）

（在古时的乐府中，有称作"辞"的，有称作"曲"的，其实"辞"就是乐曲的歌词，而"曲"则是与歌词相配的乐曲。）

In the early *yuefu* poems, some are named *ci*, and also some named *qu*. In fact, *ci* means lyrics written for music, whereas *qu* is musical tunes set to accompany lyrics. (Liu Xizai: *Overview of Literary Theories*)

◎宋元之间，词与曲一也。以文写之则为词，以声度之则为曲。（宋翔凤《乐府余论》）

（宋元之时，词和曲是同一个东西，用文句写出来就是词，给它谱上音乐就是曲。）

During the Song and Yuan dynasties, *ci* and *qu* were one and the same thing. When written with words, they were *ci*; when composed with music, they were *qu*. (Song Xiangfeng: *Epilogue to Yuefu Poetry*)

cíqǔ 词曲

_Ci_ (Lyric) and _Qu_ (Melody)

词（可以配乐歌唱的长短句诗体）和曲（可以配乐歌唱的韵文体）两种文学体式的并称，在《四库全书》列于集部最末（曲更是有类无目），这是因为在古人的文学观念中，以诗文为正统，认为诗文可以表现较为正式的内容，而词曲则仅被看作展示个人才情的末技。此外，"词曲"并称有时还用来指戏曲和说唱。

_Ci_ (词 a form of poetry with long or short verses which can be set to music and sung) and _qu_ (曲 a form of rhyming compositions which can be set to music and sung) are a combined appellation for two kinds of literary styles. In _Complete Library of the Four Branches of Literature,_ they are listed at the very end of the "Collections" section (_Qu_ is a sub-genre and is not listed in the table of contents). This is because according to the literary views of ancient scholars, poetry and essays were the only accepted tradition to express important ideas. To write in the form of _ci_ (lyric) and _qu_ (melody) was only seen as a minor skill showing a person's talent. Sometimes, the combined appellation _ciqu_ also refers to traditional opera and genres of performances featuring speaking and singing.

引例 Citation：

◎词曲二体，在文章、技艺之间。厥品颇卑，作者弗贵，特才华之士，以绮语相高耳。（《四库全书总目提要·集部·词曲类》）

（词和曲这两种体式，在文章和才艺之间。它们的地位很低，创作者也不看重它们，只是有才华的人以华丽词句用来相互标榜罢了。）

Ci and qu are genres falling between essay and performing skills. They are not highly regarded, and even their authors do not prize them. They are no more than rhetoric with which people show off their literary talent to each other! (*Complete Library of the Four Branches of Literature*)

cuòcǎi-lòujīn 错彩镂金

Gilded and Colored

涂饰彩色，雕镂金银。形容艺术作品雕饰华美。用于文学作品，主要指诗歌辞藻华丽，讲究技巧。在审美境界上，"错彩镂金"不如"芙蓉出水"高妙："错彩镂金"注重外在形态，处于审美表象阶段；而"芙蓉出水"超越表象，直达本体，是审美意趣的自然呈现。

The term is used to describe an excessively exquisite artistic work as if it were an object painted in bright colors and inlaid with gold and silver. In the literary context, it refers to poems written in a highly rhetorical style. Aesthetically, what is "gilded and colored" is considered undesirable, and the style of "lotus rising out of water" is preferred. The former focuses only on external form and appearance, whereas the latter, as a natural presentation of aesthetic ideas, penetrates appearances and brings out the essence.

引例 Citations：

◎延之尝问鲍照己与灵运优劣，照曰："谢五言如初发芙蓉，自然可爱；君诗若铺锦列绣，亦雕缋（huì）满眼。"（《南史·颜延之传》）

（颜延之曾经询问鲍照，自己的作品和谢灵运的作品相比哪个更好，鲍照说："谢灵运的五言诗像刚出水的荷花，自然可爱；您的诗像铺开的锦绣，满眼都是雕饰彩绘。"）

Yan Yanzhi asked Bao Zhao, "Whose works are better, mine or Xie Lingyun's?" Bao said, "Xie's five-word-to-a-line poems are as natural and lovely as lotus having just risen out of water in bloom, while yours are like embroidery embellished with colored decorations." (*The History of the Southern Dynasties*)

◎丹漆不文，白玉不雕，宝珠不饰，何也？质有余者，不受饰也。（刘向《说苑·反质》）

（红色的漆不需要花纹，纯白的玉不需要雕琢，珍贵的明珠不用装饰，为什么呢？本身已非常完美的东西，无需再装饰。）

Red lacquer needs no decorated patterns, white jade needs no carving, and precious pearls need no adornment. Why? Because they are too good to be worked on. (Liu Xiang: *Garden of Stories*)

dàdào-zhìjiǎn 大道至简

Great Truth in Simple Words

越普遍、越根本的道理、原则或方法其实越是浅易简便。"大道"指的是自然、社会的普遍法则以及人们对待自然、治理社会的根本原则，"简"即浅易、简明、简便。它用于治国理政及社会管理等方面，主要有两层含义：其一，越普遍、越根本的道理就应该越简明浅易，便于人们掌握并付诸实施；其二，"大道"并不是远离人世的某种高高在上的原理，它的道理、功用就蕴含在人们的伦常日用之中，只要透过纷繁的表层现象，寻流讨源，就可以抓住事物的本质和规律，以简驭繁。

The most popular and most fundamental truths, principles, and methodologies tend to be expressed in simple words and are easy to understand. *Dadao* (大道) means great truth, or universally applicable laws governing nature and society, or the fundamental principles for people to follow in treating nature and governing society. The Chinese character *jian* (简) means simple, concise, and easy. The term is often used to describe the governance of a state and management of society. It has two primary meanings. First, it means that the most popular and fundamental truths should be expressed in simple words so that ordinary people can easily understand and put them into practice. Second, *dadao* is not something separate and far away from reality. Rather, it is a practical ethical principle which is easy for people to follow in their daily lives. As long as one sees through the seemingly complicated superficialities and traces the source of things, one will be able to grasp the fundamental truths, discover the basic rules, and comprehend them in spite of the complexity.

引例 Citations：

◎博文约礼，由至著入至简，故可使不得叛而去。（张载《正蒙·中正》）
（博通文献知识，用礼约束自己，由最显明之处入手而达到最简单易行的境地，就可使自己不背离中正之道。）

He is able to keep himself to the right path if he has an excellent command of extensive literary knowledge, constrains himself with ritual propriety, and starts from the most obvious point to arrive at the most convenient situation. (Zhang Zai: *Enlightenment Through Confucian Teachings*)

◎盖道至易至简、至近至平常……故夫日用庸平，人皆不知其为道。（杨简《慈湖诗传》卷六）

（大抵道最浅易也最简便、最切近也最平常……就体现在人们每天的寻常生活之中，但人们都不知道这就是道。）

All great truths are most plain and easy to understand and most common in people's everyday life… as such, people do not think them as truths. (Yang Jian: *Cihu's Commentary on The Book of Songs*)

◎《易》之所以广大者，以其能变通也；所以变通者，阴阳二物而已；所以为阴阳者，至易而不难知，至简而不难能也。（项安世《周易玩辞》卷十三）（《周易》之所以广大无边，是因为它的变化无穷；《周易》之所以变化无穷，是因为有阴阳二气罢了；之所以归为阴阳二气，是因为阴阳最浅易而不难知晓，最简便而不难做到。）

The Book of Changes is boundless and limitless, through the ever changing nature it offers. The reason why *The Book of Changes* offers infinite changes is attributable to the two kinds of *qi*: yin and yang. The reason why everything can be traced to the two kinds of *qi*, yin and yang, is that the theory of yin and yang is easy to understand and implement. (Xiang Anshi: *Expounding the Theories of The Book of Changes*)

dàqiǎo-ruòzhuō 大巧若拙

Exquisite Skill Looks Simple and Clumsy.

极致的灵巧、技巧看上去就像质朴拙笨一样。最杰出的灵巧一定是浑然天成而非人工刻意雕琢的。出自《老子》。老子提倡纯任自然、无为才能无不为，反对一切形式的卖弄。后用来指文艺创作中的最高技巧与境界。在文艺理论中，大巧若拙并不是"以拙为巧"或完全排斥工巧，而是摒弃过分修饰和刻意追求工巧，提倡朴素自然的浑融之美。它代表了艺术美和艺术技巧的最高境界。大巧若拙是中国古代书法、绘画、园林等艺术形式的共同追求。

The term means that ingenuity and skill at their best look simple and clumsy. The greatest ingenuity should be something completely natural and that it has not been painstakingly worked on. The term comes from the book *Laozi*. Laozi the philosopher believed that everything should be in keeping with nature. He advocated non-action and was against any form of excessive act. Later, the term came to mean the highest possible level of skill and perfection in artistic and literary creation. In Chinese literary theory, "exquisite skill looks simple and clumsy" does not mean the clumsier the better, nor is it a rejection of skill. Rather, it rejects excessive embellishment and over-pursuit of the exquisite, and encourages well-founded simplicity and naturalness. The phrase represents the highest possible level of perfection in artistic beauty and skill and is also what the people in pre-modern China strove to achieve in calligraphy, painting, gardening, and other forms of art.

引例 Citation：

◎大直若屈，大巧若拙，大辩若讷。(《老子·四十五章》)
（最直的反而像是弯曲一样，最灵巧反而像是笨拙一样，最好的口才反而像不善言辞一样。）

The truly straight will appear crooked; the truly skillful will appear clumsy; the truly eloquent will appear impeded. (*Laozi*)

dàtǐ / xiǎotǐ 大体 / 小体

The Major Organ and the Minor Organs

孟子（前372？—前289）对心与感觉器官的称谓，用于对大人与小人的区分。耳、目等感觉器官为"小体"，耳目之官不具备思考与辨别的能力，因此在与外物的接触中易受外物牵引。人如果仅仅依循于"小体"，则会陷于物欲，是为小人。心为"大体"，心天生具有思考与辨别的能力。人如果能够确立"大体"的主导性，则可以通过心的作用，发现并不断扩充心中固有的善端，不为物欲所蒙蔽，是为大人。

Referring to the heart and the sensory organs, this term was used by Mencius (372?-289 BC) to differentiate between men of virtue and petty men. Sensory organs such as the ears and eyes are called "minor organs" because they lack a capacity for thought and for cognition, and are hence easily directed by externalities when they come into contact with the latter. If a man were to only rely on his "minor organs," he would be a captive of material desires and therefore become a petty man. The heart is the "major organ" which is naturally endowed with the capacity for thought and cognition. If a man is able to establish a dominant role for his "major organ," then through the actions of his heart, he will be able to continually increase its inherent goodness and not have his judgment clouded by material desires, and thereby become a man of virtue.

引例 Citation：

◎公都子问曰："钧是人也，或为大人，或为小人，何也？"孟子曰："从其大体为大人，从其小体为小人。"（《孟子·告子上》）

（公都子问道："同样是人，有些是君子，有些是小人，是什么原因呢？"孟子回答："依循于大体的成为君子，依循于小体的是小人。"）

Gongduzi asked, "We are all humans, so why are some men of virtue while others are petty men?" Mencius replied, "Those who follow their major organ become men of virtue, while those who follow their minor organs become petty men." (*Mencius*)

dàyòng 大用

Maximal Functioning

最大的运用。本义指道在外部世界的各种呈现即是道之最大的显现和运用。道家认为内在的道是主宰外部世界变化的根本，客观世界的各种形态都由作为内在本质的道所造成，是体用统一的结果。唐代司空图（837—908）《二十四诗品》将这一术语引入文学评论，目的是强调诗歌意象丰富多彩的美实际上是作品内在精神与外在形态的统一。人们进行诗歌创作与鉴赏时必须领略现象与本质之美的和谐一致。

Maximal functioning means that all kinds of appearances of Dao in the external world are the greatest manifestation and functioning of Dao. Daoist scholars believe that the internal Dao determines the basis for changes in the external world, and that all kinds of forms in the objective world derive from the active, innate nature of Dao, the result of unity of substance and function. In "Twenty-four Styles of Poetry," Sikong Tu (837-908), a literary critic in the Tang Dynasty, made this notion a term of literary criticism to highlight the view that the rich and colorful imagery in poetry represents unity of the internal spirit of the work and its external shape. In poetry writing and appreciation, one should focus on the harmony between the appearance and the essence.

引例 Citation：

◎大用外腓（féi），真体内充。反虚入浑，积健为雄。（司空图《二十四诗品·雄浑》）

（大道呈现于外显得雄浑阔大，真实的本体则充满于内。唯有返回虚静，内心才能到达浑然之境；积蓄精神力量，笔力才能雄放豪健。）

The grand appearance is an external manifestation of Dao, while the true vitality permeates itself internally. Reverting to a tranquil void, one may gain fullness and amass inner strength, and he will produce powerful works. (Sikong Tu: Twenty-four Styles of Poetry)

dānqīng 丹青

Painting in Colors

丹和青是中国古代绘画常用的两种颜色，早期中国画常用丹砂、青䨼（huò）一类矿物颜料"勾线填色"，因而用"丹青"代指绘画。代表性的丹青作品有西汉马王堆一号墓帛画，北魏、隋唐时期的敦煌壁画等。后丹青逐渐为水墨所代替。由于丹青颜色鲜艳绚丽，且不易褪色，古代用丹册纪勋、青史纪事。史家多以丹青比喻一个人功勋卓著，永载史册，不会磨灭。

Dan (丹 cinnabar) and *qing* (青 cyan) were two colors frequently applied in traditional Chinese painting. Cinnabar is red and cyan is bluish green. In early times, Chinese paintings often used minerals such as cinnabar and cyan to draw lines or fill in colors. Hence the term *danqing* (丹青) made from the combination of *dan* and *qing* could stand for painting in general. Representative works of this kind included silk paintings unearthed at Tomb No.1 of Mawangdui of the Han Dynasty as well as the Dunhuang frescoes of the Northern Wei period and the Sui and Tang dynasties. Later, colors made from cinnabar and cyan were gradually replaced by ink and wash. Partly because of their bright, contrastive colors, and partly because mineral colors do not deteriorate appreciably over time, people used red-character books to record merits and bluish-green-character books to record historical events. Historians often use *danqing* to refer to a man's outstanding, indelible work that deserves to be put down in history.

引例 Citations：

◎［顾恺之］尤善丹青，图写特妙。谢安深重之，以为有苍生以来未之有也。（《晋书·顾恺之传》）

（顾恺之尤其擅长绘画，画出来的人物奇特精妙。谢安非常器重他，认为他是自有人类以来从未有过的杰出画家。）

Gu Kaizhi was particularly skillful in painting. The figures he portrayed are amazingly vivid and lovely. Xie An held him in high esteem, and regarded him as superior to all other artists, past and present. (*The History of the Jin Dynasty*)

◎故丹青画其形容，良史载其功勋。（曹丕《与孟达书》）

（是以画家画下他的相貌，史家记载他的功劳。）

Thus a painter portrays a person's physical features, just as a historian records his accomplishments. (Cao Pi: A Letter to Meng Da)

dànbó 淡泊

Quiet Living with No Worldly Desire

恬淡宁静。最初指清心寡欲、平和恬淡的一种人生态度。道家主张"淡",认为淡而无味才是至味,这种思想对于"淡泊"审美观念的形成有较大影响。从魏晋时代开始,淡泊被运用于审美领域,指平和清淡的艺术美感与风格,与浓艳富丽相对。淡泊不是淡而无味,是指经过了提纯、熔炼,宁静而空灵,平淡而有深远的韵味。

This term was first used to mean to lead a quiet, peaceful life with few worldly desires. Daoism advocates blandness, believing that lack of flavor is the best possible flavor. It was highly influential in the creation of the aesthetic concept of blandness and quiet living. Beginning in the Wei and Jin dynasties, the term was used in aesthetics, referring to a peaceful and mild artistic beauty and style, as opposed to rich, loud and splendid beauty. The term does not mean insipid with no taste at all; what it refers to is a purified, refined, quiet and ethereal taste, a mild yet profound tone and flavor.

引例 Citations:

◎夫君子之行,静以修身,俭以养德,非淡泊无以明志,非宁静无以致远。(诸葛亮《诫子书》)

(君子的行为,以内心安宁来修养身体,以节俭朴素来培养品德,不恬淡宁静就无法拥有崇高的志向,不安宁平静就无法实现远大的目标。)

In conducting himself, a man of virtue should maintain inner peace to cultivate his moral character and be frugal to cultivate virtue. Unless he is indifferent to fame and fortune, he cannot have aspirations; unless he stays calm and quiet, he cannot reach afar. (Zhuge Liang: Letter of Warning to My Son)

◎独韦应物、柳宗元发纤秾于简古，寄至味于澹泊，非余子所及也。（苏轼《书黄子思诗集后》）

（只有韦应物、柳宗元，在质朴高古中蕴含细腻丰厚，在平静雅淡中蕴含无穷的韵味，是其他人远远不及的。）

Only Wei Yingwu and Liu Zongyuan far exceeded others, because in their poetry, rich delicacy dwells in vintage simplicity and nuanced profundity in serene composure. (Su Shi: Postscript to *Selected Poems of Huang Zisi*)

dànbó-míngzhì, níngjìng-zhìyuǎn 淡泊明志，宁静致远

Indifference to Fame and Fortune Characterizes a High Aim in Life, and Leading a Quiet Life Helps One Accomplish Something Lasting.

　　淡泊名利才能明确自己的志向，心神宁静才能达到远大的目标。"淡泊"，恬淡寡欲，不重名利；"宁静"，安宁恬静，不为外物所动；"致远"，到达远处，即实现远大目标。这是古代中国人所追求的自我修养的一种境界，其核心是对待名利的态度。它希望人们不要贪图名利，为名利所累；要始终胸怀远大理想，专心一意地为实现远大理想而努力。

This saying, with the attitude to fame and fortune at its core, refers to a way in which people in ancient China sought to practice self-cultivation. People should not be greedy for fame and fortune and be burdened by such greed. Instead they ought to cherish noble ideals and work heart and soul to achieve them.

引例 Citations：

◎是故非澹薄无以明德，非宁静无以致远，非宽大无以兼覆，非慈厚无以怀众，非平正无以制断。(《淮南子·主术训》)

（所以，不淡泊名利就不能彰明道德，不心神宁静就不能达到远大目标，不心胸广阔就不能兼蓄并包，不慈爱宽厚就不能安抚大众，不公平中正就不能掌控决断。）

Hence, unless he is indifferent to fame and fortune, he cannot demonstrate his virtue; unless he stays calm and quiet, he cannot reach afar; unless he is magnanimous, he cannot learn from others and be inclusive; unless he is kind and warm-hearted, he cannot embrace the people; unless he is even-handed and righteous, he cannot take control and make decisions. (*Huainanzi*)

◎非淡泊无以明志，非宁静无以致远。(诸葛亮《诫子书》)

（不恬淡宁静就无法拥有崇高的志向，不安宁平静就无法实现远大的目标。）

Unless he is indifferent to fame and fortune, he cannot have aspirations; unless he stays calm and quiet, he cannot reach afar. (Zhuge Liang: *Letter of Warning to My Son*)

dāngháng 当行

Professionalism

内行，在行。最初用于诗歌评论，指诗歌创作完全契合诗歌的体制规范。后发展成为中国古典戏曲理论的重要术语。主要含义有二：其一，指戏曲语言质朴自然、浅显通俗，符合人物性格并适合舞台表演；其二，指戏曲中的角色创造及故事情景，真实传神，具有强烈的艺术感染力，能让观众沉浸其中。在明代戏曲理论中，"当行"经常与"本色"连用，能当行、具本色的戏曲作品就是上乘佳作。

The expression was first used in poetry criticism to mean that a poem fully met poetic stylistic standards. It later became an important term in Chinese classical operatic theory. It has two meanings. One is that the language used by a character in a play is simple, natural, easy to understand, and appropriate for the character. The other is that characters and plot of the play are true to life with a strong artistic attraction. In Ming-dynasty operatic theory, "professionalism" and "being true to life" are often used together to describe outstanding opera works.

引例 Citations：

◎曲始于胡元，大略贵当行不贵藻丽。（凌濛初《谭曲杂札》）

（戏曲从元代开始，大体上重视通俗浅显，不重视辞藻华丽。）

Beginning in the Yuan Dynasty, professional simplicity, rather than flowery rhetoric, has gained popularity as an operatic style. (Ling Mengchu: Miscellaneous Notes on Opera)

◎行家者随所妆演，无不摹拟曲尽，宛若身当其处，而几忘其事之乌有，能使人快者掀髯，愤者扼腕，悲者掩泣，羡者色飞。是惟优孟衣冠，然后可与于此。故称曲上乘，首曰当行。（臧懋（mào）循《元曲选·序二》）

（行家根据自己所扮演的角色，无不摹拟相似，曲尽其妙，好像完全置身其中，忘记了所表演的事情并不是真的，能够让人在快乐时胡须张开，在愤怒时握紧手腕，在悲伤时掩面哭泣，在羡慕时神色飞动。只有优孟那样的艺人，才能达到这种效果。因此，说到戏曲上乘，首要的标准就是当行。)

Professional actors can play their roles so vividly as if they were the characters themselves, forgetting that the story is fictional. Their performances can make viewers so happy that their beards will fly up, or make them so angry that they will wring their wrists, or make them so sad that they will sob, or inspire them so much that they will become thrilled. Only artists like Youmeng can create such effect. Therefore, for an opera to be outstanding, it first and foremost must be professional. (Zang Maoxun: *Selected Works of Yuan Opera*)

dàojìtiānxià 道济天下

Support All People by Upholding Truth and Justice

以"道"拯救、帮助天下的人。"道"指道理、道义，也可以是某种学说、思想等；"济"即救助，使人免于困苦；"天下"指世间所有的人。"道济天下"包含两层意思：其一，"道"的价值有无、大小就是看它于天下人是否有益。其二，君子特别是知识分子应该将自己所主张或掌握的"道"用于天下，用于经世济民。和"经世致用"一样，"道济天下"实质代表中国传统知识分子治学立世的终极目标与人格理想，体现了中国传统知识分子追求真理、坚持真理、关注社会民生以及"以天下为己任"的人文情怀和道德境界。

The term means to save and help all people through upholding truth and justice. *Dao* (道) here refers to truth and justice, and also to particular thought or doctrine. *Ji* (济) means relieving or helping people out of difficulties or sufferings. *Tianxia* (天下) refers to everything under heaven, and particularly all people. Therefore, this phrase contains two meanings. First, the value of any particular Dao depends on whether it serves the interests of the people. Second, people of virtue, and intellectuals in particular, should apply Dao they have learned to serve the people and use the ancient classics they have studied to meet present needs. Much like the idea of "studying ancient classics to meet present needs," this notion of "supporting all people by upholding truth and justice," represents the ultimate goal and ideal character of the traditional Chinese intellectuals in their pursuit of knowledge. It also embodies the compassion and moral standards of the traditional Chinese intellectuals as they pursue and uphold truth, care about the livelihood of the people, and take upon themselves the responsibility for the world.

引例 Citations：

◎知周乎万物，而道济天下，故不过。(《周易·系辞上》)
([圣人的]智慧广大，遍及万物，而他的道德又能救助天下的人，所以不会犯错。)

Sages won't make mistakes, for they have endless wisdom about everything under heaven and their virtues help all people in the world. (*The Book of Changes*)

◎文起八代之衰，而道济天下之溺；忠犯人主之怒，而勇夺三军之帅。(苏轼《潮州韩文公庙碑》)
(韩愈所倡导的古文，彻底改变了八朝相沿的衰败文风；他所高扬的儒家之道，拯救了天下人沉溺于佛老思想而带来的精神困境，他忠诚进言不惜触怒皇帝，他独闯叛军营帐其勇气可折服三军主帅。)

The classical style of writing known as *guwen* advocated by Han Yu revived the literary style in decline during the eight dynasties; and Confucianism he promoted lifted the people out of their mental plight caused by their blind faith in Buddhism and Daoism. He gave candid advice to the emperor without fearing of angering him. He courageously broke into the camp of the rebel army alone, winning the respect of the commander-in-chief. (Su Shi: Eulogy for the Temple of Han Yu in Chaozhou)

dédào-duōzhù, shīdào-guǎzhù 得道多助，失道寡助

A Just Cause Enjoys Abundant Support While an Unjust Cause Finds Little.

奉行道义，支持的人就多；违背道义，支持的人就少。"道"即道义、正义。中国人自古推崇道义，认为道义是决定战争或事业成败的根本力量。只有奉行道义，才能赢得内部的团结一致、赢得民心，取得战争或事业的最后胜利；否则就将不得人心，从而陷入孤立无援的境地，归于失败。它是中华"德政"思想与"文明"精神的具体体现。

The Chinese phrase *dedao* (得道) or "obtaining Dao" here refers to having "a just cause." Since ancient times Chinese people have had a high esteem for justice and have thought of justice as a decisive factor determining success or failure in war and other enterprises. Only by upholding justice can one achieve internal unity and popular support, which are essential for the success of a war or a cause; otherwise, popular support is lost and the ruler or leader becomes too isolated and helpless to succeed. This is a specific expression of the Chinese notion of "governance based on virtue" and the spirit of "civilization."

引例 Citations：

◎域民不以封疆之界，固国不以山溪之险，威天下不以兵革之利。得道者多助，失道者寡助。寡助之至，亲戚畔之。多助之至，天下顺之。以天下之所顺，攻亲戚之所畔，故君子有不战，战必胜矣。（《孟子·公孙丑下》）
（使百姓定居下来不能依靠划定疆域的界限，保护国家不能依靠山河的险要，威慑天下不能依靠兵器的锐利。奉行道义，支持的人就多；违背道义，支持的人就少。支持的人少到了极致，连亲戚都背叛他。支持的人多到了极致，天下人都归顺他。凭借天下人都归顺的力量，攻打连亲戚都背叛的人，所以君子不战则已，战就一定取得胜利。）

The people are not confined by boundaries, the state is not secured by dangerous cliffs and streams, and the world is not overawed by sharp weapons. The one who has Dao enjoys abundant support while the one who has lost Dao finds little support. When lack of support reaches its extreme point, even a ruler's own relatives will rebel against him. When abundant support reaches its extreme point, the whole world will follow him. If one whom the whole world follows attacks one whose own relatives rebel against him, the result is clear. Therefore, a man of virtue either does not go to war, or if he does, he is certain to win victory. (*Mencius*)

◎桀纣之失天下也，失其民也；失其民者，失其心也。得天下有道，得其民，斯得天下矣。得其民有道，得其心，斯得民矣。得其心有道，所欲与之聚之，所恶勿施尔也。（《孟子·离娄上》）
（桀和纣所以失去天下，是因为失去百姓；所谓失去百姓，就是失去了民心。得到天下有规律，得到百姓，就能得到天下。得到百姓有规律，得到民心，就能得到百姓。得到民心有规律，百姓想得到的，就替他们聚积起来；百姓所厌恶的，就不要施加于他们身上，如此罢了。）

Jie and Zhou lost all under heaven because they lost the people. They lost the people because they lost the people's hearts. There is a way to win all under heaven: if you win the people, you win all under heaven. There is a way to win the people: if you win their hearts, you win the people. There is a way to win their hearts: amass for them what they desire, do not impose on them what they detest, and it is as simple as that. (*Mencius*)

déxìngzhīzhī 德性之知

Knowledge from One's Moral Nature

由心的作用而获得的超越于感官经验的认识，与"见闻之知"相对。张载（1020—1077）最先区分了"见闻之知"与"德性之知"。宋儒认为，人对生活世界的认识是通过两种不同方式实现的。通过目见、耳闻所获得的认识，是"见闻之知"；通过内心的道德修养所获得的认识，则是"德性之知"。"德性之知"不依赖于感官见闻，并超越于"见闻之知"，是对于生活世界的根本认识。

The term refers to knowledge derived from the functioning of the mind, which, in contrast to "knowledge from one's senses," transcends knowledge obtained through the sensory organs. Zhang Zai (1020-1077) was the first to differentiate between "knowledge from one's senses" and "knowledge from one's moral nature." Confucian scholars of the Song Dynasty felt that people gained knowledge about the world in which they lived in two ways. Knowledge obtained from seeing and hearing was "knowledge from one's senses," whereas knowledge obtained through moral cultivation of the mind was "knowledge from one's moral nature." "Knowledge from one's moral nature" was not reliant on the sensory organs; it transcended "knowledge from one's senses" and was fundamental knowledge about the world in which one lived.

引例 Citation：

◎见闻之知，乃物交而知，非德性所知；德性所知，不萌于见闻。（张载《正蒙·大心》）

（见闻之知，乃是耳目与外物接触而获得的知识，并不是德性之知；德性之知，不产生于见闻所得的经验知识。）

Knowledge from one's senses comes from contact with external objects and is not knowledge from one's moral nature. Knowledge from one's moral nature does not come from sensory perceptions. (Zhang Zai: *Enlightenment Through Confucian Teachings*)

diǎnyǎ 典雅

Classical Elegance

指文章典范雅正。最初指写文章要有经典依据，文章的思想内容应纯正高尚，以经典文献特别是儒家的义理规章作为审美规范，后侧重指文章的文辞和风格高雅优美而不浅俗艳浮。其后，"典雅"这一术语又逐步融入道家自然恬淡、超尘出世的审美意蕴，如司空图（837—908）在《二十四诗品》中用"落花无言，人淡如菊"来描述"典雅"，就很接近道家自然恬淡的风格。

This term refers to a type of writing that is classically elegant. Originally, it meant that a piece of writing should be modeled on ancient classics, express pure and noble ideas, and follow classical literary styles by using Confucian doctrines for aesthetic guidance. Later, the term shifted to emphasize elegant diction and style that were free from vulgarity and frivolity. Later still, it gradually incorporated Daoist aesthetic views, suggesting natural tranquility and spiritual transcendence. For example, in "Twenty-four Styles of Poetry," Sikong Tu (837-908) described classical elegance as being "as quiet as falling flower petals and as modest as unassuming daisies," which is close to the simple, relaxed, and natural style advocated by Daoist scholars.

引例 Citations：

◎ 典雅者，熔式经诰，方轨儒门者也。(刘勰《文心雕龙·体性》)

(所谓典雅，就是取法于儒家经典文献，遵照儒家义理章法。)

Classical elegance is achieved by emulating the Confucian classics and following Confucian doctrines in literary creation. (Liu Xie: *The Literary Mind and the Carving of Dragons*)

◎ [徐干] 著《中论》二十篇，成一家之言，辞义典雅，足传于后。(曹丕《与吴质书》)

(徐干著《中论》二十篇，成一家之言，文辞有典据而高雅，足以传之于后世。)

Xu Gan wrote his 20-chapter book *Discourses That Hit the Mark*, establishing a distinctive theory of his own. The carefully-researched, well-elaborated and highly elegant writings deserve to be passed on to future generations. (Cao Pi: *A Letter to Wu Zhi*)

dǐng 鼎

Ding (Vessel)

古代用于烹煮食物的器物，也是重要的礼器。相传夏禹铸九鼎，象征九州，成为夏、商、周三代传国的重要器物，被视作王位合法性、权威性的物证。鼎多以青铜铸成，一般两耳三足或四足。三足喻"三公"（古代中央掌管全国行政、司法、军事最高权力的三个官职），四足喻"四辅"（古代天子身边的四个辅佐）。秦代以后，鼎作为实物逐渐失去王权象征意义，但"鼎"字仍被用于指王位、帝业或国家政权，也被赋予"显赫""盛大""尊贵"等义。

Ding was a vessel to cook food and was also used as an important ritual object in ancient times. Legend has it that Emperor Yu of the Xia Dynasty had nine *ding*s cast, symbolizing the nine regions in the country. *Ding* was regarded as embodying the legitimacy and authority of the throne during the three dynasties of Xia, Shang, and Zhou. *Ding* was mostly cast in bronze, usually with two ears and three or four legs. The three legs stood for the "three chief ministers" (the three most powerful official positions in ancient times in charge of national civil administration, the judiciary, and military affairs). The four legs stood for the four advisors to the emperor. After the Qin Dynasty, *ding* gradually lost its function as a symbol of royal authority, but the word *ding* was still used to refer to the royal throne, the monarchy, or state power. It was also given the meaning of "glory," "grandeur," and "dignity."

引例 Citations：

◎鼎者，宗庙之宝器也。（《汉书·五行志中之上》）

（鼎是宗庙中象征王位的祭器。）

The *ding* was a vessel symbolizing the highest authority in an ancestral temple. (*The History of the Han Dynasty*)

◎论逆臣则呼为问鼎。（刘知几（jī）《史通·叙事》）

（论及逆臣，就称之为"问鼎"。）

A minister who wanted to seize the throne was referred to as one who inquired about the *ding*. (Liu Zhiji: *All About Historiography*)

dòngjìng 动静

Movement and Stillness

事物存在的两种基本状态。就具体事物的存在状态而言，事物或运动或静止。两种状态是对立的，但也是相互依赖、相互转换的。但对于事物恒常的或本质的存在状态，古人则有着不同的认识。儒家认为，"动"才是事物更根本的存在状态。天地万物处于永恒的变化与运动之中。道家则认为，运动的具体事物起始于"静"，最终也要归于"静"。佛家则主张，事物本质上都是静止的，人们所看到的运动变化只是虚幻的假象。

The term refers to two fundamental states in the existence of things, namely, movement and stillness. These two kinds of states are antithetic, but they also rely on each other and change into each other. Ancient Chinese had different views about the constant or the intrinsic state of the existence of things. Confucian scholars believed that "movement" was the fundamental state of existence of things, and that all things under heaven and on earth were in perpetual change and motion. Daoist scholars held that concrete things in motion were originally still, and that they would eventually return to stillness. Buddhists maintained that things were inherently all still and that the movements and changes people saw were just illusionary.

引例 Citations:

◎动静有常，刚柔断矣。(《周易·系辞下》)

（事物的动静变化有其规则，由此断定事物的刚柔。）

There is a fundamental rule governing the movement and stillness of things, which determines if a thing is firm or gentle. (*The Book of Changes*)

◎凡动息则静，静非对动者也。(王弼《周易注》)

（凡是运动的事物停息则归于静，本体的静不是与具体事物的动相对应的。）

When things stop to move, there is stillness. Fundamental stillness does not correspond to movement in concrete things. (Wang Bi: *Annotations on The Book of Changes*)

◎必求静于诸动，故虽动而常静。(僧肇《肇论·物不迁论》)

（必须在各种事物的变动中探究静的本质，那么虽然表面是变动的，但本质上却是恒常静止的。）

One should explore stillness in every movement. By doing so, he can see that beneath movement there lies constant stillness. (Seng Zhao: *Treatise of Seng Zhao*)

duō xíng bù yì bì zì bì 多行不义必自毙

He Who Repeatedly Commits Wrongdoing Will Come to No Good End.

不合道义的事情干多了，必定自取灭亡。"不义"指行为违背道义。

"义"是社会普遍遵循的道德规范;"义"又与"宜"相通,指循理合宜。中华民族自古重"义",小到个人,大到国家,都强调行事以"义"为依据。凡是违法乱纪、祸国殃民、作恶多端的人,都不会有好下场。

A person who repeatedly acts immorally will only end up in total failure. *Buyi* (不义) is an act which violates the principles of *yi* (义 righteousness). Righteousness is the moral code broadly accepted by a society; it is synonymous with *yi* (宜 propriety), meaning the observance of what is fit and proper. The Chinese have championed righteousness since ancient times, believing that all acts, whether those of individuals or of a nation, should be based on righteousness. Anyone who breaks laws, harms the country or the people, or commits numerous acts of wrongdoing will come to no good end.

引例 Citation:

◎多行不义必自毙。子姑待之。(《左传·隐公元年》)

(不合道义的事情干多了,必定自取灭亡。您姑且等着吧。)

He who repeatedly commits wrongdoing will come to no good end. You just wait and see! (*Zuo's Commentary on The Spring and Autumn Annals*)

fánrù 繁缛

Overly Elaborative

指诗文辞藻华丽、描写详尽(与"简洁"相对)。西晋时期以陆机(261—303)为代表,在文学创作上出现了追求辞藻富丽、文思繁密的倾向。陆机的作品多用典故和对偶句,讲求精雕细琢,文辞繁复华美,同时也有不够清新流畅的弊病。至南朝齐梁时期，刘勰（465？—520？或532？）《文心雕龙》把"繁缛"列为文章八种风格之一。

This term refers to a literary writing style that is ornate and flowery in diction and excessively detailed and exhaustive in description, in contrast to being "simple and concise." The tendency to write elaborately about an idea in ornate language first emerged in the Western Jin Dynasty, represented by the writings of Lu Ji (261-303). His works were rich in allusions and antitheses, meticulous in diction and description, and elaborate and ornate in style. At the same time, these writings suffered from a lack of clarity and novelty. During the Qi and Liang of the Southern Dynasties, this overly elaborative style was listed as one of the eight major literary styles in Liu Xie's (465?-520? or 532?) *The Literary Mind and the Carving of Dragons*.

引例 Citations：

◎繁缛者，博喻酿采，炜烨枝派者也。（刘勰《文心雕龙·体性》）
（所谓繁缛，就是博用比喻，辞藻丰富，文采灿烂，如同树木多枝、河流派分一样。）

An overly elaborative style is known for its profuse use of allusions and ornate language to generate literary effect, like a tree branching out and a river forking into multiple streams. (Liu Xie: *The Literary Mind and the Carving of Dragons*)

◎或藻思绮合，清丽千眠。炳若缛绣，凄若繁弦。（陆机《文赋》）
（写作有时是辞藻华美、文思交会，清新富丽，色彩绚烂。光彩耀目如同装饰繁盛的锦绣，凄切流连如同繁复多变的弦乐。）

Sometimes, one can employ flowery language in writing that makes the idea and language of a work mutually reinforcing, creating a refreshing and appealing effect in a consistently colorful style. It can be dazzling and gorgeous like a piece of exquisitely adorned brocade, or sentimental and lingering like an intricate piece of plaintive string music. (Lu Ji: The Art of Writing)

fēnggǔ 风骨

Fenggu

指作品中由纯正的思想感情和严密的条理结构所形成的刚健劲拔、具强大艺术表现力与感染力的神韵风貌。其准确含义学界争议较大，但大致可描述为风神清朗，骨力劲拔。"风"侧重指思想情感的表达，要求作品思想纯正，气韵生动，富有情感；"骨"侧重指作品的骨架、结构及词句安排，要求作品刚健遒劲、蕴含丰富但文辞精炼。如果堆砌辞藻，过于雕章琢句，虽然词句丰富繁多但内容很少，则是没有"骨"；如果表达艰涩，缺乏情感和生机，则是没有"风"。风骨并不排斥文采，而是要和文采配合，才能成为好作品。风骨的高下主要取决于创作者的精神风貌、品格气质。南朝刘勰（465？—520？或532？）《文心雕龙》专门列有《风骨》一篇，它是我国古代文学批评史上首篇论述文学风格的文章。

This term refers to powerful expressiveness and artistic impact that come from a literary work's purity of thoughts and emotions, as well as from its meticulously crafted structure. Despite some difference in interpreting the term, people tend to agree that *fenggu* (风骨) can be understood as being lucid and fresh in language while sturdy in structure. *Feng* (风) means "style," which emphasizes that a literary work should be based on pure thoughts, vivid impressions, and rich emotions so as to produce an effect of powerful expressiveness. *Gu* (骨) means "bones" or proper structure, figuratively. It stresses the impact of structure and sentence order, requiring a piece of writing to be robust, vigorous, profound, and yet succinct. If a piece of work is wordy and overly rhetorical but weak in content, then it lacks the impact of a "proper structure," no matter how flowery its expressions are. If such writing is awkward in delivery and has no emotions and vitality, then it lacks expressiveness in "style." *Fenggu* does not preclude, but rather combines with linguistic elegance in order to create a piece of good work. Good command of *fenggu* depends on the personality and dispositions of the author. In *The Literary Mind and the Carving of Dragons*, Liu Xie (465?-520? or 532?) of the Southern Dynasties devoted a chapter to the discussion of *fenggu*, which is the first essay on writing style in the history of classical Chinese literary criticism.

引例 Citations：

◎文章须自出机杼，成一家风骨，何能共人同生活也！（《魏书·祖莹传》）（文章必须有自己的构思布局，有自己作品的风骨，如何能与他人同一个层次！）

A piece of writing must have its own structure, and its own *fenggu*, that is, expressiveness in style and sturdiness in structure. How can it ever be the same as the writings of other writers! (*The History of Northern Wei*)

◎捶字坚而难移，结响凝而不滞，此风骨之力也。（刘勰《文心雕龙·风骨》）（字句锤炼确切而难以改动，读起来声音凝重有力而不滞涩，这就是风骨的魅力。）

The charm of *fenggu* in a literary work derives from deliberate and precise diction that is hard to alter, and from powerful and controlled sounds that do not sound awkward when read out. (Liu Xie: *The Literary Mind and the Carving of Dragons*)

◎若能确乎正式，使文明以健，则风清骨峻，篇体光华。(刘勰《文心雕龙·风骨》)

(倘若能够定好正确合适的文体，使文采鲜明而又气势刚健，那么自可达到风神清新明朗，骨力高峻劲拔，通篇文章都会生发光彩。)

Once a good and appropriate style is set to make the writing lucid and vigorous, it will produce the effect of being pure, clear and powerfully impressive, making the writing both remarkable and appealing. (Liu Xie: *The Literary Mind and the Carving of Dragons*)

fēngjiào 风教

Moral Cultivation

原义为教育感化，后侧重指风俗教化，即文学艺术作品对改变世情民风所起的教育感化作用。源于《毛诗序》，是儒家关于艺术功能论的重要范畴之一。"风教"强调诗歌、音乐对于人的思想感情的教育引导作用，认为统治者能够用诗歌、音乐为工具，自上而下地传达某种理念、教育感化民众，收到移风易俗的功效。"风教"观念影响深远，从先秦时代的诗歌、音乐到近代的文学艺术作品，大多遵循这一思想，是儒家伦理教育观念的具体体现，也是文学家、艺术家社会责任感的体现。但如果艺术作品过于强调风教，会造成理念先行、理念大过形象，损害艺术作品的审美价值。最好的方式是寓教于乐，让文艺作品在潜移默化中影响人心。

Originally, this term meant to educate and influence people. Later, it came to refer to the function of shaping customary social practices, namely, the educational role of literary and artistic works in changing social behaviors and popular culture. Originating from "Introductions to *Mao's Version of The Book of Songs*," the term is one of the important concepts of the Confucian school on the function of the arts. It believes that poetry and music have a role to play in shaping people's mind, reflecting the notion that rulers can educate and influence the general public by imparting a particular ideology in a top-down fashion, thereby achieving the desired effect of cultivating the general culture. The influence of this concept is far-reaching; it has impacted much of artistic creation in China, all the way from the poetry and music of the pre-Qin period to literary and artistic works in the modern times. It not only reflects the Confucian view on moral education, but also imparts a sense of social responsibility on writers and artists. However, if an artistic work overemphasizes moral cultivation, it runs the risk of placing ideology before artistic form, thus compromising its aesthetic value. The right way is to embed teaching in entertainment and let a literary or artistic work exert its influence on social mentality in a subtle and imperceptible way.

引例 Citations：

◎《关雎》……风之始也，所以风（fēng）天下而正夫妇也。故用之乡人焉，用之邦国焉。风，风（fēng）也，教也，风（fēng）以动之，教以化之。(《毛诗序》)

(《关雎》……是《诗经》十五国风的开始，也是教化的开始，它的功用就是教育感化民众、端正夫妇的行为。风教既可应用于乡间百姓，也可应用于国家层面。风，就是风吹万物，就是教育，像风吹万物一样打动人，以教育感化人。)

"Guan Ju," the first ballad in a collection from the fifteen states in *The Book of Songs,* marks the starting point where moral education was conscientiously pursued. Its purpose was to educate and influence the general public and ensure the proper behavior between spouses. Moral cultivation can be conducted both at the individual and national levels. *Feng* (ballad), with its original meaning of wind, allegorically means to persuade and influence people like the wind touches everything. (Introductions to *Mao's Version of The Book of Songs*)

◎尝谓有能观渊明之文者，驰竞之情遣，鄙吝之意祛，贪夫可以廉，懦夫可以立。岂止仁义可蹈，抑乃爵禄可辞。……此亦有助于风教也。（萧统《〈陶渊明集〉序》）

（我曾经说过，凡是能读懂陶渊明文章的人，就会抛开争名逐利的想法，去除贪鄙吝啬的念头，贪婪的人可以廉洁，懦弱的人可以自立。不只是能够实践仁义，还能辞却一切官爵俸禄。……这就是有助于风俗教化。）

I once said that those who truly understand the writings of Tao Yuanming would be able to resist the temptations of personal fame and gains, and overcome greedy or stingy inclinations. With such understanding, a corrupted person would seek to attain integrity, and a timid one to become self-reliant; people would not only practice benevolence, but also decline offers of any official positions and salaries… This is how moral cultivation can be promoted. (Xiao Tong: Preface to *Collection of Tao Yuanming's Works*)

fúróng-chūshuǐ 芙蓉出水

Lotus Rising Out of Water

美丽的荷花从水中生长出来。形容清新、淡雅、自然之美，与"错彩镂金"的修饰之美构成对比。魏晋六朝时崇尚自然，与这种审美理想一致，在艺术创作方面，人们欣赏像"芙蓉出水"一般的天然清新的风格，注重主观意趣的自然呈现，反对过分雕琢修饰。

The term of lotus rising out of water describes a scene of freshness, quiet refinement and natural beauty, in contrast to "gilded and colored" embellishments. During the Wei and Jin dynasties, people valued nature and favored this aesthetic view. In their artistic creations, they pursued the natural and fresh style like lotus rising out of water. They sought natural presentation of their ideas and were opposed to excessive ornamentation.

引例 Citations：

◎谢诗如芙蓉出水，颜如错彩镂金。（钟嵘《诗品》卷中）

（谢灵运的诗清新自然，像荷花出水；颜延之的诗歌修饰雕琢，像涂绘彩色、雕镂金银。）

Xie Lingyun's poems are natural and refreshing like lotus rising out of water, whereas Yan Yanzhi's poems are elegantly embellished, like gilding an object and adding colors to it. (Zhonq Ronq: *The Critique of Poetry*)

◎清水出芙蓉，天然去雕饰。（李白《经乱离后天恩流夜郎忆旧游书怀赠江夏韦太守良宰》）

（从清水中生长出的荷花，自然天成没有雕饰。）

It is like a lotus rising out of clear water: natural and without embellishment. (Li Bai: To Wei Liangzai, the Governor of Jiangxia, Written While Thinking of My Friends on My Way into Exile at Yelang Following the War)

gāngróu-xiāngjì 刚柔相济

Combine Toughness with Softness

刚与柔两种手段互相调剂、配合。"刚"与"柔"是指人和事物的两种相反的属性。就执政理事而言,"刚"指强硬、严厉,"柔"指温柔、宽宥,"刚柔相济"相当于"恩威并施"。"刚柔"被认为是"阴阳"的具体表现。"刚"与"柔"之间的对立与调和是促成事物运动变化的根本原因。具体到政策、法令的制定与实施及社会或企业的管理,刚与柔需保持某种均衡状态。

Gang (刚) and *rou* (柔) are two mutually complementary measures. They refer to two opposite properties or qualities that objects and human beings possess. In the realm of governance, *gang* means being tough and stern, while *rou* means being soft and lenient, and the term means to combine tough management with gentle care. *Gang* and *rou* are considered to be a concrete manifestation of yin and yang. Their mutual opposition and accommodation are the causes of change. When formulating and implementing policies and decrees or managing a society or an enterprise, there must be a certain balance between *gang* and *rou*.

引例 Citations:

◎孔子云:"礼以行之,孙(xùn)以出之。"外柔内刚、刚柔相济而不相胜者,万事之所以成也。(郑善夫《答道夫》)

(孔子说:"按礼的要求实践,用谦逊的言辞说出。"外柔内刚、刚柔相济而不是一方压过另一方,万事就能获得成功。)

Confucius said: "One must perform righteousness according to the rules of propriety and speak in humility." One should be soft and gentle without, while tough and firm within, and should combine toughness with softness, without trying to overpower the other side. This is the way to achieve success in doing everything. (Zheng Shanfu: Letter in Reply to Daofu)

◎ 凡为将者，当以刚柔相济，不可徒恃其勇。（罗贯中《三国演义》第七十一回）

（凡担任大将的人，都应该用刚柔相济，不可只是凭着自己的勇猛行事。）

All generals must combine toughness with softness, and should not act with personal prowess only. (Luo Guanzhong: *Romance of the Three Kingdoms*)

gē 歌

Song

一种篇幅短小、可以吟唱的韵文作品，是集文学、音乐甚至是舞蹈于一体的可以歌唱的文学艺术创作形式。在中国古代，歌与诗的区别是："歌"能入乐歌唱，"诗"通常不入乐歌唱。广义的歌包括了童谣、民谣；狭义的歌与谣有所区别：有固定曲调和音乐伴奏的是歌，没有固定曲调的清唱为谣。歌大多为民间创作的民歌，如汉乐府《长歌行》、北朝民歌《敕勒歌》等；也有小部分是由文士等个人创作的作品，如刘邦（前256或前247—前195）的《大风歌》、李白（701—762）的《子夜吴歌》等。"歌"属于中国古代诗歌艺术的早期形态，古人一般将其归入乐府诗，现在则与诗合称"诗歌"。

Songs are a kind of short, rhyming composition. It is a form of artistic creation combining literature, music, and even dance which can be sung. The difference between songs and poems in ancient China is that the former could be made into music and sung, whereas the latter could not. In a broad sense, the term includes children's ballads and folk ballads. In a narrow sense, songs and ballads are different. Songs have a fixed melody and musical accompaniment, while ballads do not. Songs were created mostly by folk musicians, such as "A Slow Song" of the Han Dynasty and the folk song "Song of the Chile" of the Northern Dynasties. A small number of songs, however, were written by members of the literati, like "Ode to the Great Wind" by Liu Bang (256 or 247-195 BC) and "The Midnight Melody of the Land of Wu" by Li Bai (701-762). Songs are one of the early forms of ancient Chinese poetic art and were generally classified as *yuefu* (乐府) poetry in ancient China. In modern times, they are called poetic songs as a part of poetry.

引例 Citation：

◎曲合乐曰歌，徒歌曰谣。(《诗经·魏风·园有桃》毛传)
(配上曲调、有音乐伴奏的叫做"歌"，没有固定曲调的清唱叫做"谣"。)

Words sung with the accompaniment of music are called songs, and mere singing and chanting are called ballads. (*Mao's Annotations on The Book of Songs*)

gégù-dǐngxīn 革故鼎新

Do Away with the Old and Set Up the New

革除旧事物，创建新事物。"革"与"鼎"是《周易》中的两卦。在《易传》的解释中，革卦下卦象征火，上卦象征泽。火与泽因对立冲突不能维持原有的平衡状态，必然发生变化。因此革卦意指变革某种不合的旧状态。鼎卦下卦象征木，上卦象征火。以木柴投入火中，是以鼎烹饪制作新的食物。因此鼎卦象征创造新事物。后人承《易传》之说，将二者合在一起，代表一种主张变化的世界观。

Do away with the old and set up the new. *Ge* (革) and *ding* (鼎) are two trigrams in *The Book of Changes*. In *Commentary on The Book of Changes*, it is explained that the lower *ge* trigram symbolizes fire and the upper *ge* trigram symbolizes water. Since fire and water are opposed and in conflict, and they cannot keep an original state of equilibrium, changes are bound to occur. Consequently, the *ge* trigram implies change of an unsuitable old state of affairs. The lower *ding* trigram symbolizes wood and the upper *ding* trigram symbolizes fire. When people throw the wood into the fire, they can cook their food in a *ding*. Thus, the *ding* trigram signifies the creation of new things. Following the doctrine in *Commentary on The Book of Changes*, later people combined the two together to represent an outlook advocating changes.

引例 Citation：

◎革，去故也；鼎，取新也。(《周易·杂卦》)
（革卦，意味着革除旧事物；鼎卦，意味着创建新事物。）

Ge trigram signifies doing away with the old; *ding* trigram symbolizes setting up the new. (*The Book of Changes*)

gōng shēng míng, lián shēng wēi 公生明，廉生威

Fairness Fosters Discernment and Integrity Creates Authority.

处事公正才能明察是非，做人廉洁才能树立威望。这是明清两代一些正直廉洁的官吏用以自戒的座右铭。"公"即公正无私；"明"即明察是非，有很强的分辨力和判断力；"廉"即廉洁；"威"即威望，有令人信服的公信力。时至今日，它仍是执政者应当遵循的最重要的为官准则：执政当公平公正，在国家法律和规定程序的框架内进行；官员当以身作则，廉洁自律，克己奉公，不可以权谋私。

Only by being fair can one distinguish between right and wrong; only with moral conduct can one establish authority. These mottoes were used as reminders by upright officials of the Ming and Qing dynasties. *Gong* (公) means fairness and opposing pursuit of selfish interest. *Ming* (明) means discernment, namely, the ability to distinguish right from wrong. *Lian* (廉) means free from corruption. *Wei* (威) means authority or credibility. Today, these teachings have remained important principles which office holders should abide by. They mean that governance should be exercised in a fair and just way and within the framework of laws and regulatory procedures of the state. Officials should lead by example, have moral integrity and be self-disciplined; they should put public interests above their own and not use their power to pursue personal gain.

引例 Citation：

◎吏不畏吾严而畏吾廉，民不服吾能而服吾公。公则民不敢慢，廉则吏不敢欺。公生明，廉生威。（年富《官箴》刻石）

（官吏不害怕我的严厉但害怕我廉洁，百姓不信服我的才能但信服我的公正。我公正，百姓就不敢轻慢；我廉洁，官吏就不敢欺瞒。处事公正才能明察是非，做人廉洁才能树立威望。）

Officials have a sense of awe towards me not because of my being strict with them, but because of my upright conduct. People accept my authority not because of my ability, but because of my fairness. If I am fair, people will not dare to disobey my order; if I am morally upright, officials will not dare to deceive me. Only by being fair can one distinguish between right and wrong; only with moral integrity can one establish authority. (Nian Fu: Mottoes for Officials, from a stone carving)

hàoránzhīqì 浩然之气

Noble Spirit

　　盛大而充盈于生命之中的正直之气。孟子（前372？—前289）认为"浩然之气"是与道义相匹配的，由内而生，非得自于外。个人能够坚守善道，反省自身行事能无愧于心，"浩然之气"就会自然发生并逐渐充盈。一旦养成"浩然之气"，行正义之事便能果决勇敢而无所疑虑。

Noble spirit is a powerful source of cultivating integrity in one's life. In Mencius' (372?-289 BC) view, it goes hand in hand with morality and justice and originates from within rather than from without. If one lives an ethical life and regularly conducts soul searching, he will be imbued with noble spirit and will willingly stand up for what is right.

引例 Citation：

◎ "敢问何谓浩然之气？"曰："难言也。其为气也，至大至刚，以直养而无害，则塞于天地之间。其为气也，配义与道。无是，馁也。"（《孟子·公孙丑上》）

（"请问什么叫浩然之气呢？"孟子回答说："难以言说。浩然之气极其强大、极其刚正，用正义去培养它而不去伤害它，它就会充满于天地之间。作为一种气，它是与义和道相匹配的。没有义和道的相配，气就会疲弱无力。"）

"May I ask what noble spirit is?" "It is something hard to describe," Mencius answered. "As a vital force, it is immensely powerful and just. Cultivate it with rectitude and keep it unharmed, and it will fill all the space between heaven and earth. Being a vital force, noble spirit becomes powerful with the accompaniment of righteousness and Dao. Without righteousness and Dao, noble spirit will be weak and frail." (*Mencius*)

jìtuō 寄托

Entrust One's Thoughts and Feelings to Imagery

指诗歌作品通过形象化而寄寓作者的主观认识或感受，并能激发读者的联想。"寄"是寄寓一定的思想内容和个人情志，"托"是托物兴咏。是清代常州词派提出的一个文学术语。张惠言（1761—1802）主张词要继承《诗经》的比兴、讽喻传统。周济（1781—1839）进而认为，初学写词应力求有寄托，以提升作品意蕴、激发读者的思考和艺术想象；待入门后，则不能拘于寄托，而要言意浑融，无迹可寻。这一主张实质是反对观念先行，强调文学自身的特性，对于当时的文学创作有积极的导向作用。

The term refers to the entrusting of the poet's subjective understanding or sentiments to imagery in poetic works. It can also stir responsive appreciation of the reader. *Ji* (寄) means having a specific thought or individual feelings, and *tuo* (托) means giving expression to such thought or feelings through the channel of an object. It is a literary term first used by a group of *ci* (词 lyric) poets from Changzhou during the Qing Dynasty. Zhang Huiyan (1761-1802) stressed that lyric writing should follow the tradition of analogies, associations and allegories in *The Book of Songs*. Zhou Ji (1781-1839) further suggested that an aspiring poet should entrust his thought to imagery in order to raise the artistic appeal of his work and stimulate the imagination of the reader. After having established himself, however, the poet should not be bound by the technique of entrusting to imagery; rather, his words and sentiments should blend seamlessly. This view emphasized the primacy of nature of literature as opposed to the primacy of concept and provided a new guidance for literary creation at the time.

引例 Citation：

◎夫词，非寄托不入，专寄托不出。(周济《宋四家词选目录序论》)
(作词，如果没有寄托，就很难深入；如果只专力于寄托，就不能意出词外。)

When writing *ci* poetry, one cannot effectively express one's thoughts and sentiments without entrusting them to imagery. On the other hand, overreliance on imagery will make it hard for one to clearly express his idea. (Zhou Ji: Preface to *Contents of Selected Poems of Four Poets of the Song Dynasty*)

jiànlì-sīyì 见利思义

Think of Righteousness in the Face of Gain

在面对利益之时，首先思考、分辨利益的获取是否符合道义。是儒家用以处理义利关系的准则。对利益的追求与对道义的坚守之间常存冲突。人们往往会因为贪图私利而忽视道义，行背德违法之事。针对这种情况，孔子（前551—前479）提出了"见利思义"的主张，倡导人们应该在道义的原则之下谋求利益。知晓道义的是君子，一味追求利益的是小人。

When faced with gain one should first consider and distinguish whether the obtainment of gain is in accord with morality. This is a Confucian criterion for dealing with the relation between righteousness and gain. Between the pursuit of gain and the upholding of morality a conflict has long existed. Because people more often than not may covet personal gain and overlook morality, their actions may go against virtue and violate the law. Against this kind of situation Confucius (551-479 BC) advanced the stand of "thinking of righteousness in the face of gain," proposing that people should strive for gain on the basis of the principle of morality. He who knows morality is a man of virtue, and he who blindly pursues gain is a petty man.

引例 Citation：

◎见利思义，见危授命，久要（yāo）不忘平生之言，亦可以为成人矣。(《论语·宪问》)

（看见利益时思考该不该得，遇到危险时肯付出生命，经过长久的穷困而不忘记平日的诺言，也可以说是成人了。）

He who when faced with gain thinks of righteousness, who when confronted with danger is ready to lay down his life, and who does not forget a past promise despite enduring poverty, may be considered a true man! (*The Analects*)

jiànwénzhīzhī 见闻之知

Knowledge from One's Senses

由耳、目等感官与外物接触而获得的认识，与"德性之知"相对。张载（1020—1077）最先区分了"见闻之知"与"德性之知"。宋儒认为，人对生活世界的认识是通过两种不同方式实现的。通过目见耳闻所获得的认识，即是"见闻之知"。"见闻之知"是人的认识所不可缺少的。但"见闻之知"不足以穷尽对事物的认识，也无法获得对世界本体或本原的认识。

The term refers to knowledge derived from contact between externalities and one's sensory organs such as the ears and eyes, in contrast to "knowledge from one's moral nature." Zhang Zai (1020-1077) was the first to differentiate between "knowledge from one's senses" and "knowledge from one's moral nature." Confucian scholars of the Song Dynasty felt that people acquired knowledge about the world in which they lived in two ways. Knowledge obtained from seeing and hearing was "knowledge from the senses," which was an essential part of human knowledge. However, it was not a complete picture, nor could it provide an understanding of the original source or ontological existence of the world.

引例 Citation：

◎闻见之知，非德性之知，物交物则知之，非内也。(《二程遗书》卷

二十五）

（闻见之知，不是德性之知，感官与外物相接触则获得了对外界的认知，并非由内心而生。）

Knowledge from one's senses is not knowledge from one's moral nature. It comes from contact with external objects and not from the inner workings of the heart. (*Writings of the Cheng Brothers*)

jiànxián-sīqí 见贤思齐

When Seeing a Person of High Caliber, Strive to Be His Equal.

遇见有德才的人，就要想着努力向他看齐。"贤"指德才兼备的人；"齐"是看齐，达到同样的水平。"见贤思齐"是孔子（前551—前479）对自己学生的教导，后成为世人修身养德、增进才智的座右铭。其主旨在于鼓励人们善于发现他人长处，激发内心的自觉，主动向道德、学问、技能等比自己强的人学习看齐，从而不断进步。它体现了中华民族一心向善、积极进取、自强不息的精神。

This term means that when you see a person of high caliber, you should try to emulate and equal the person. *Xian* (贤) refers to a person of virtue and capability; *qi* (齐) means to emulate and reach the same level. This was what Confucius (551-479 BC) taught his students to do. The term has become a motto for cultivating one's moral character and increasing one's knowledge. The main point of this term is to encourage people to discover the strengths of others and take initiative to learn from those who are stronger than themselves in terms of moral qualities, knowledge, and skills so as to make constant progress. The term embodies the Chinese nation's spirit for good, enterprise, and tenacious self-renewal.

引例 Citations：

◎子曰："见贤思齐焉，见不贤而内自省也。"（《论语·里仁》）
（孔子说："遇见有德才的人，就要想着努力向他看齐；遇见德才不好的人，就要在内心反省自己［是否有同样的缺点］。"）

Confucius said, "When you see a person of virtue and capability, you should think of emulating and equaling the person; when you see a person of low caliber, you should reflect on your own weak points." (*The Analects*)

◎君子博学而日参（cān）省乎己，则知明而行无过矣。（《荀子·劝学》）
（君子广泛学习并且每天坚持自我参验、反省，就可以做到智慧明达而行为不会有错了。）

Men of virtue, who study extensively and reflect on themselves every day, become wise and intelligent and are free from making mistakes. (*Xunzi*)

jiàngǔ-zhījīn 鉴古知今

Review the Past to Understand the Present

以过去、历史为镜鉴，可以了解现在并预知未来。也说"鉴往知来""知古鉴今"。"鉴"本指镜子，引申为借鉴、参照，审察、考察。所谓"鉴古""鉴往""知古"主要指总结历史上朝代、国家兴衰成败的经验教训，考察历史人物的言行事迹以及是非善恶，来为现实的国家治理和个人的道德修养服务。"知今""鉴今""知来"则是了解现在，以现在为鉴，预知未来。

古代执政者为了使自己的决策符合国情、民情，具一定合理性，非常注重从历史中吸取经验教训，以避免重蹈覆辙。它包含着对于历史的现实意义和现实的历史景深的双重关注。与"前事不忘，后事之师"意思接近。

Reviewing the past helps us understand the present and predict the future. It is also said that "reviewing the past we understand the future" and "knowing the past we understand the present." The Chinese word *jian* (鉴) can mean "mirror" and hence to "review the past" as if in a mirror, "understand the past," or "gain knowledge of the past." The lessons of the rise and fall of dynasties and states, the words and deeds of historical figures, as well as right and wrong, and good and evil, help govern the country and improve personal morality. "Understanding the present," "reviewing the present," or "understanding the future" means predicting the future based on the present. The rulers of antiquity saw it as extremely important to draw lessons from history in order to avoid past mistakes and justify their policies by making them conform to the needs of the country and people. The concept of "reviewing the past to understand the present" stresses both the practical significance of history and the historical depth of things present. It is similar to the concept that "past experience, if not forgotten, is a guide for the future."

引例 Citations：

◎监前世之兴衰，考当今之得失，嘉善矜恶，取是舍非。(司马光《进〈资治通鉴〉表》)

(察看前代政权的兴衰，考察当今的得失，赞美善德，戒惧恶行，采纳正确做法，放弃错误做法。)

It is advisable to review the rise and fall of previous dynasties and the achievements and failures of the present dynasty, to commend the good, condemn the evil, and adopt what is right and discard what is wrong. (Sima

Guang: Memorial on *History as a Mirror*)

◎知往见今，驱曹荡吴，非同小可也。(无名氏《太平宴》第一折)

(了解过去，作为现在的镜鉴，驱除和消灭曹魏、孙吴，这是了不起的事业。)

It is of great importance to review knowledge of the past to help understand the present, expel the invasion of the State of Wei and wipe out the State of Wu. (*A Peace Banquet*)

jìnxīn 尽心

Exert One's Heart / Mind to the Utmost

充分体认和发挥内心固有的善端。"尽心"是由孟子(前372？—前289)提出的一种道德修养方法。"尽心"需要发挥心所具有的思考能力，发现人心中固有的善端，并将其作为人之所以为人的本质特征，进而充分培养、发挥心中的善端，最终实现仁、义、礼、智的德行。心中的善端是天赋予人的本性，因此通过"尽心"就能够知晓人的本性，并通达于天。

"Exerting one's mind to the utmost" means one should fully understand and extend one's innate goodness. It is a way of moral cultivation advocated by Mencius (372-289 BC). To do so, one needs to develop one's capability of thinking, discover the goodness inherent in the mind and then fully nurture this innate human character, eventually realizing the moral qualities of benevolence, righteousness, rites and social norms, and wisdom.

引例 Citations：

◎孟子曰："尽其心者，知其性也。知其性，则知天矣。存其心，养其性，所以事天也。"（《孟子·尽心上》）

（孟子言："能做到尽心的人，能知晓其本性。能知晓人的本性，则能够知晓天。保持自己的本心，培养自己的本性，就是对待天命的方法。"）

Mencius said, "He who does his utmost knows his nature. Knowing his nature, he knows his inborn moral nature. Preserving his mind and nurturing his nature is the way to deal with the mandate of heaven. (*Mencius*)

◎尽心，谓事物之理皆知之而无不尽。（《朱子语类》卷六十）

（尽心是指能够知晓事物所具有的理而毫无遗漏。）

Exerting one's mind to the utmost means knowing the laws of all things, with nothing left out. (*Categorized Conversations of Master Zhu Xi*)

kōnglíng 空灵

Ethereal Effect

指文学艺术作品中所呈现的飘逸灵动的艺术境界与风格。与"充实"相对。空灵并非空虚无物，它并不脱离具体的物象描写，而是通过有限的艺术形象达到无限的艺术意境，追求一种象外之意、画外之情，给人留下想象发挥的空间，如诗文中不着形迹、不堆砌辞藻和意象，绘画中较少使用浓墨重彩等。空灵用笔洗练，重在传达神韵，具有空灵特点的作品澄澈透明、飘逸灵动，能使人体悟到自由超脱的审美愉悦。

This refers to an open, free, and flexible style of a work of art; it is the opposite of a "densely packed" work of art. Ethereal effect does not mean sheer emptiness; it does not completely avoid imagery, nor does it entirely avoid natural description. Rather its aim is to suggest unlimited possibilities for the viewer's imagination through a highly economical use of brushwork and imagery so as to pursue the "meaning that lies beyond literal form" or "associations beyond the work itself." In this way it leaves room for the viewer's imagination. For example, just as redundant description is deliberately left out of an essay or a poem, along with ponderous wording or unnecessary images, just so thick ink and heavy colors may be avoided in painting. The notion of ethereal effect values simple layout and an economical use of details, seeking to convey character and imagination. Works that make use of ethereal effect convey a wonderful lucidity, and possess openness, freedom, and natural grace. Such works enable viewers to appreciate the aesthetic joy of free imagination.

引例 Citations：

◎古人用笔极塞实处愈见虚灵，今人布置一角已见繁缛。虚处实则通体皆灵，愈多而愈不厌。（恽格《南田画跋·题画》）

（古人绘画，越是在非常具体实在的地方，用笔越有飘逸灵动的感觉。今天的人作画，才画了一角，就已看起来琐碎繁杂。在虚飘的地方用实笔，则整幅作品都显得灵动，所绘物象越多越不会让人生厌。）

When painting, classical artists made use of ethereal effect all the more where a dense collection of objects normally was required. However today's artists no sooner begin to paint than they fill the space with elaborate details. In fact, if a painter applies a few specific details strategically in the empty spaces, then the whole picture will appear more open and alive. Under the circumstances the more images he uses, the less boring the picture. (Yun Ge: *Nantian's Comments on Paintings*)

◎文或结实，或空灵，虽各有所长，皆不免著于一偏。试观韩文，结实处何尝不空灵，空灵处何尝不结实。（刘熙载《艺概·文概》）
（文章或者坚实有力，或者飘逸灵动，虽然各有各的优点，都难免偏于一个方面。试看韩愈的文章，坚实有力的地方未尝不飘逸灵动，飘逸灵动的地方未尝不坚实有力。）

Some essays are written in a substantive style, whereas others feature an ethereal style. Although these two kinds of writing have their respective merits, they are each lopsided in their own way. But if one reads Han Yu's essays, he will find that they are a perfect combination of substantive content and ethereal effect. (Liu Xizai: *Overview of Literary Theories*)

kuàngdá 旷达

Broad-mindedness / Unconstrained Style

指诗歌作品中所体现的超然物外、旷放通达的胸襟和艺术风格。是作者通达的人生观及平和心态与作品艺术形象的高度融合。具有旷放性情的作者，多因世事坎坷或社会动乱而落魄或退隐，往往以诗文抒写胸臆，反映在诗歌作品中，既有对世事物情超旷出尘的人生警悟，也有愤世嫉俗、傲岸不羁的真情流露。它的渊源可以追溯到儒家有为和道家顺其自然的思想及魏晋名士超尘脱俗、开朗达观的人生态度。既不逃避世俗，也不贪恋名利，事理通达，心境开阔。唐代司空图（837—908）将其提升为一个诗学、美学术语，强调作品风格与作者心态及人生观的统一，意在倡导一种超脱旷达的人生观与审美心态。

The term means broad-mindedness and a totally unconstrained artistic style in poetic works. It presents a perfect union of the author's outlook on life, his peaceful mind, and the artistic form of his work. A broad-minded writer was often disheartened, who went into seclusion, caused either by frustrations countered in life or social turmoil, and he would naturally seek to express his emotion in literature. As reflected in his writings, such a writer possessed a keen insight into the vicissitudes of worldly affairs. Being cynical and indignant, he also revealed such feelings of disdain for the world and its ways in his writings. The origin of this attitude can be traced back to the Confucian concept of proactivity and the Daoist proposition of following the nature, as well as to the open and cultured way of life characteristic of famous scholars of the Wei and Jin dynasties. Such a writer would not shy away from the worldly, but neither would he cling to fame and wealth. He was completely reasonable in attitude and tolerant in mood. Sikong Tu (837-908), a literary critic in the Tang Dynasty, used this term to assess poetic and aesthetic achievement by emphasizing the unity of the style of a work and the mental attitude and the view about human life on the part of the author. The idea is to promote a view about life and an aesthetic attitude that is open-minded and uplifting.

引例 Citation:

◎生者百岁，相去几何。欢乐苦短，忧愁实多。何如尊酒，日往烟萝。花覆茅檐，疏雨相过。倒酒既尽，杖藜行歌。孰不有古，南山峨峨。（司空图《二十四诗品·旷达》）

（人的一生不过百年，寿命长短能差几何。欢乐时光总苦短促，忧愁日子其实更多。哪里比得上手持酒樽，每日在烟绕藤缠的幽静处畅饮。那鲜花覆盖的茅檐下，细雨疏疏飘忽访顾。壶中酒已经喝完，拄着藜杖漫步唱歌。谁没有死的那一天？只有终南山才会巍峨长存。）

There are no more than a hundred years in a man's life, so what difference does it make whether it is long or short! Joys are painfully brief, but sorrows are numerous. There is nothing like holding a goblet of drink, strolling in the mist and the quiet and shady garden, or watching rain drizzling down the thatched eaves covered with flowers! After finishing the drink, I will just take another stroll and sing! Who can escape from one's last day? Only the Zhongnan Mountains will forever stay lofty. (Sikong Tu: Twenty-four Styles of Poetry)

lǐshàngwǎnglái 礼尚往来

Reciprocity as a Social Norm

礼注重相互往来和互惠。"礼"即礼制，"尚"即崇尚、注重。指人与人之间、组织与组织之间、国家与国家之间的交往互动，其中隐含着对等互惠的人际、国际关系思想。有时也表示用对方对待自己的态度和方式去对待对方，类似于"即以其人之道，还治其人之身"。

Etiquette requires reciprocity and mutual benefit. It refers to contacts and interactions between individuals, between organizations, and between nations and implies equality and mutual benefit in interpersonal and inter-state relations. Sometimes, it also means that one should treat the other party in the way the other party treats you. It is similar to "Treating the other person the way he treats you."

引例 Citation：

◎礼尚往来。往而不来，非礼也；来而不往，亦非礼也。人有礼则安，无礼

则危。(《礼记·曲礼上》)

(礼注重的是往来互惠。我给人礼物而人未回馈，这是违反礼的；人给我礼物而我未回赠，这也是不合乎礼的。人做事符合礼就会平安无事，违反礼就会危及自身。)

Etiquette values reciprocity and mutual benefit. It would go against it if someone who has received a gift does not reciprocate such goodwill. When one acts according to such etiquette, one will enjoy peace. Without it, one will cause trouble. (*The Book of Rites*)

lǐyī-fēnshū 理一分殊

There Is But One *Li* (Universal Principle), Which Exists in Diverse Forms.

作为最高范畴的"理"存在于不同事物之中或呈现为不同形态。"理一分殊"是宋明理学家对"理"的存在形式的一个重要理解。由于"理"的含义不同，"理一分殊"的意义也有所差别：其一，就万物本体或本原之"理"而言，每一事物都禀受了这个"理"。每一事物之"理"并不是分有"理"的一部分，而是禀受了"理"的全部意义。其二，就万物所遵循的普遍法则而言，普遍之"理"在具体事物之中表现为不同的原理。每一事物之"理"是普遍之"理"的具体表现。"理一"保证了世界的统一性，而"分殊"则为事物的多样性与等级秩序提供了依据。

Being a supreme domain in terms of principle, *li* (理) exists in different things and manifests itself in different forms. "There is but one *li*, which exists in diverse forms" – this is an important way in which the Song- and Ming-dynasty thinkers viewed the forms in which *li* exists. As *li* has different meanings, its one-and-diverse composition is also interpreted in different ways. First, as the origin of universe in an ontological sense, *li* runs through all things. The *li* of each thing is not a part of *li*, rather, it is endowed with the full meaning of *li*. Second, representing the universal law governing all things, the universal *li* expresses itself in the form of different guiding principles in specific things. The *li* of each thing or being is a concrete expression of the universal *li*. The concept of *li* being one and same ensures unity of the world, whereas its diversity provides the basis for multifarious things and hierarchical order.

引例 Citations：

◎万物皆有此理，理皆同出一原，但所居之位不同，则其理之用不一。(《朱子语类》卷十八)

(万物都具有这个理，万物所具之理都源自一处，但其所处的情境不同，因此理的具体运用和呈现样式就有不同。)

Li (universal principle) runs through all things, which is derived from one source. But as *li* is present in different things, its functions and forms vary. (*Categorized Conversations of Master Zhu Xi*)

◎盖人物之生，受气之初，其理惟一；成形之后，其分则殊。(罗钦顺《困知记》卷上)

(人和事物在禀气初生之际，他们所具有的理是唯一的；而具有了各自的形体之后，理的具体表现又各不相同。)

When a person or thing comes into being and is endowed with *qi*, or vital force, he or it is governed by only one *li* (universal principle). However, once a person or thing gains a specific physical form, the *li* embodied expresses itself in different ways. (Luo Qinshun: *Knowledge Painfully Acquired*)

nèiměi 内美

Inner Beauty

内在的美好性情与品德。初见于屈原（前340？—前278？）《离骚》，指先天禀赋的美德，由家族遗传及早期环境造就。与之相随的是"修能"，即初明事理后自觉自主地进行品德修养，并培养更多的才能。后来，用这一术语强调作者应该具有内在的美好性情与品德，高尚伟大的人格决定高尚伟大的文学。

Inner beauty means a fine disposition and moral character. It first appeared in *Li Sao* by Qu Yuan (340?-278? BC), referring to an inherited innate moral character which was further fostered in one's early living environment. On this basis acquired competence develops, which is achieved when one, after gaining initial understanding of the principles of things, consciously improves his moral character through self-cultivation, and strengthens one's abilities. Later this term is used to emphasize that an author should possess an inner fine disposition and moral character, and that noble and great literature can only derive from a noble and great character.

引例 Citations：

◎纷吾既有此内美兮，又重之以修能。（屈原《离骚》）
（我天生拥有这么多美好的品德，又继续培养自己的卓越才能。）

Armed with such moral qualities given me by birth, I continue to develop competence. (Qu Yuan: *Li Sao*)

◎文学之事，于此二者，不可缺一。然词乃抒情之作，故尤重内美。（王国

维《〈人间词话〉删稿》)

(文学创作这件事,要求内在品质和杰出才能两方面,缺一不可。而词是抒发性情的作品,所以尤其注重内美。)

In literary creation, one must have both moral standard and outstanding capabilities. Neither is dispensable. As *ci* lyrics give expression to emotions, one must focus on bringing out the inner beauty. (Wang Guowei: *Poetic Remarks in the Human World [The Deleted Part]*)

pǐjí-tàilái 否极泰来

When Worse Comes to the Worst, Things Will Turn for the Better.

坏的到了尽头或极点,就会转而变好。"泰"和"否"是《周易》中的两个卦名,分别表示正面和负面意义,如通与塞、顺与逆、好与坏等。古人认为,万事万物都处在循环往复的变换过程中;在一定临界点上,事物内部所包含的对立的两个方面就会发生相互转化。"否极泰来"揭示了事物发展变化的辩证法,给困境中的人带来精神支柱和希望,使人乐观奋发,把握时机,扭转局面。辩证地看,它也是忧患意识的表征。

When worse comes to the worst, things and events at their extremes will reverse and turn for the better. *Tai* (泰) and *pi* (否), two of the hexagram names in *The Book of Changes*, represent the positive and negative aspects of things, with one unimpeded and the other blocked, one faced with favorable conditions and the other with adversity, and one good and the other bad. In the view of ancient Chinese, all things cycle around and forever change. When they reach a certain critical point, they will transform into the opposite of their extreme characteristics. The term reveals the dialectical movements of development and change. It gives moral support and hope to people experiencing difficulties, and encourages people to be optimistic, seize the opportunity, work hard, and turn things around. From a dialectical perspective, it represents a sense of preparing for the worst.

引例 Citation：

◎乾下坤上，所以为泰也；坤下乾上，所以为否也。泰者，通也；否者，塞也；泰者，辟也；否者，阖也。一通一塞、一阖一辟，如寒暑之相推，如昏明之相代，物理之常，虽天地圣人有不能逃也。（林栗《周易经传集解》卷六）

（乾下坤上，所以是泰卦；坤下乾上，所以是否卦。泰的意思是"通"，否的意思是"塞[不通]"；泰的意思是"开"，否的意思是"闭"。一"通"一"塞"、一"开"一"闭"，就像冬天与夏天、黑夜与白昼的相互更替一样，是事物很平常的现象，即便是天地和圣人也不可能逃离它的变化。）

The picture of heaven down and earth above is *tai* hexagram while that of the other way round is *pi* hexagram. *Tai* means things are smooth and unimpeded, while *pi* means things are blocked. Likewise, *tai* means "open" while *pi* means "closed." With one unimpeded and the other blocked, one open and the other closed, the two form a circle. It is a common phenomenon to replace each other regularly, like winter and summer, and day and night, moving on in cycles. Even heaven and earth, as well as sages, cannot escape from changing. (Lin Li: *Notes and Commentaries on The Book of Changes*)

piāoyì 飘逸

Natural Grace

指诗歌作品中所表现出的逍遥自适、超凡脱俗、无拘无束的审美情趣和艺术风格。作为一个诗学术语，它也集中体现了诗人思想独立、天性自由的精神气质和审美追求，及"独与天地精神往来"、自由遨游于无限时空的意境，是诗歌意境、诗人与诗中人物融为一体而呈现出的艺术风格。往往与"沉郁"的诗歌风格相对应。

Natural grace, a term for poetic study (often in contrast to the "melancholy" poetic style), refers to free and unconstrained aesthetic style and artistic appeal in poetic works. It gives expression to the imagination of the poet, the natural and free disposition of his spirit, and his pursuit of aesthetic enjoyment. When in such a state of mind, the poet is "totally absorbed in his interaction with heaven and earth," roaming freely in boundless time and space. The concept represents a poetic style in which the poet and what he portrays in his poem merge into a natural whole.

引例 Citation：

◎子美不能为太白之飘逸，太白不能为子美之沉郁。（严羽《沧浪诗话・诗评》）

（杜甫写不出李白那种自由潇洒、超凡脱俗的诗篇，李白也写不出杜甫那种深沉厚重的作品。）

Du Fu could not write as freely and unconstrained as Li Bai, while the latter did not possess the style of melancholy and profoundness typical of Du Fu's poems. (Yan Yu: *Canglang's Criticism on Poetry*)

qíwù 齐物

See Things as Equal

破除事物之间差异与对立的一种认识态度或生活方式。庄子（前369？—前286）在《齐物论》中通过对世界的变化无常的揭示，说明差异与对立的事物之间内在相通。因此在认识层面，应该从世界的相通的本质出发，视万物齐等如一，放弃自我的立场所带来的对事物的分别与好恶。心游离于事物之外，摆脱事物的限制与影响。事物之间差异与对立的表象不再构成内心乃至生命的负担。

This refers to a worldview or lifestyle that seeks to reconcile differences and contradictions among things. In "On Seeing Things as Equal", Zhuangzi (369?-286 BC) analyzes the unpredictable nature of the world to reveal that different or opposing things are inherently interconnected. In striving to understand the world, one should therefore first of all identify the interconnectedness among all things in the world, see all as equal, and abandon personal preferences, likes and dislikes. In this way, one's heart can be above all material things and free from their constraints and influences, and the differences and contradictions among things will no longer burden one's mind or one's life.

引例 Citation：

◎故齐物而偏尚之累去矣。（郭象《庄子注》卷一）

（因此能够做到齐物，则由个人偏好所带来的各种弊端都不存在了。）

Hence if we can see all things as equal, there will be no flaws brought about by our personal preferences. (Guo Xiang: *Annotations on Zhuangzi*)

qìgǔ 气骨

Qigu (Emotional Vitality and Forcefulness)

指作品的气势与骨力。多形容文学艺术作品所呈现出的刚健劲拔的精神气度和力度美。"气骨"这一术语出现于南朝,与当时的人物品评风气相呼应,用来形容诗文、书法、绘画等文学艺术作品中劲健的精神气度和内在骨力,与"风骨"含义接近,而与"风姿"(作品外在的风貌姿态)相对。

This term refers to the emotional strength and the vitality of a literary work. It was first used during the Southern Dynasties, resonating with the social practice of making comment on people. The term was used to describe the emotional vigor and forcefulness of artistic works such as poetry, essays, calligraphy, and paintings. It is similar in meaning to *fenggu* (风骨), but contrary to *fengzi* (风姿), a term meaning external elegance of an artistic work.

引例 Citations:

◎言气骨则建安为俦,论宫商则太康不逮。(殷璠(fán)《河岳英灵集·集论》)

(论气势与骨力,能与建安时期的作品相媲美;论音节与韵律,能超过太康时期的作品。)

In terms of its emotional vitality and forcefulness, the poem stands equal to works of the Jian'an Reign period; in terms of its musicality and rhythms, it surpasses the works of the Taikang Reign period. (Yin Fan: *A Collection of Poems by Distinguished Poets*)

◎观鲁公此帖，奇伟秀拔，奄有魏晋隋唐以来风流气骨。（黄庭坚《题颜鲁公帖》）

（观颜真卿这个法帖，奇特雄伟，秀美挺拔，全然具备魏晋隋唐以来的神韵气骨。）

This piece of calligraphy by Lord Lu (Yan Zhenqing) is amazing, vigorous, mellow, and forceful, fully illustrating the admirable emotional vitality and strength that characterized the style since the Wei, Jin, Sui and Tang dynasties. (Huang Tingjian: *Inscription on Yan Zhenqing's Calligraphy*)

qìzhìzhīxìng 气质之性

Character Endowed by *Qi* (Vital Force)

"气"所赋予或影响的人的本性（与"天命之性"或"天地之性"相对）。"气质之性"包含两种不同的含义：其一，指"气"赋予人的禀性。或指人的刚柔缓急的性格，或指贤愚等具有道德含义的品格。这个意义上的"气质之性"与"天命之性"共同构成了人天生所具的本性。其二，指"天理"与"气"共同影响的人性。"天理"落入有形的身体之中就会受到"气"的影响。"天理"所赋予的道德本性与身体的欲求交错在一起，即是"气质之性"。

The moral characters of humans endowed or influenced by *qi* (气) stand in contrast with "characters endowed by Heaven" or "characters endowed by Heaven and Earth." The term encompasses two meanings. First, it refers to the specific disposition of a person under the influence of *qi*, such as firmness and gentleness, patience and impatience, and wisdom and stupidity. In this sense, the "character endowed by *qi*" and the "character endowed by Heaven" together constitute a person's inborn character. Second, it means that heavenly laws and *qi* together influence a person's character. As heavenly laws are imbedded in the physical human body, they are influenced by *qi*. The interaction of moral characters endowed by heavenly laws and human desires reflects the "character endowed by *qi* (vital force)."

引例 Citations：

◎形而后有气质之性，善反之则天地之性存焉。(张载《正蒙·诚明》)
(事物凝聚成形以后就禀受了气质之性，善于复归本原则天地之性得以实现。)

Physical matters take up their shape which acquires the nature of *qi* (vital force); if we are thus good at returning to it, then the nature endowed by heaven and earth will be preserved. (Zhang Zai: *Enlightenment Through Confucian Teachings*)

◎论天地之性，则专指理言；论气质之性，则以理与气杂而言之。(《朱子语类》卷四)
(论说天地之性，则是专门就天理而言的；论说气质之性，则是就天理与气混合一体而言的。)

As for the properties of heaven and earth, they refer exclusively to heavenly laws. As for the nature of *qi*, it refers to the combination of heavenly laws and *qi*. (*Categorized Conversations of Master Zhu Xi*)

qì 器

Qi (Vessel)

实在的器物或具体的职官、身份等。"器"是有形的或可以具体描述的。每一种"器"都具有特定的形态、功用或能力。因此,"器"与"器"之间有着明确的界限和差别。但不同的"器"之中又包含着相通的"道"。"器"的存在来自于"道"且依赖于"道"。具体就人事而言,个人在自己的职分中担负着特定的责任,但又应超越具体而有限的器用,致力于对"道"的体认与遵循。

Qi (器) is a real object or a specific official, position, etc. A *qi* is something visible, or something one may describe in concrete terms. Every kind of *qi* has a specific form, function, or capability. Therefore there are clear distinctions between one *qi* and another. However, a common Dao exists in different kinds of *qi*. The existence of a *qi* is based on Dao. In terms of human affairs, an individual assumes a particular responsibility suited to his position; but he should go beyond his specific capabilities and strive to adhere to and obtain Dao.

引例 Citations：

◎形而上者谓之道,形而下者谓之器。(《周易·系辞上》)
(未成形质者称为"道",已成形质者称为"器"。)

What is above form is called Dao, and what is under form is called "an object." (*The Book of Changes*)

◎子曰："君子不器。"(《论语·为政》)
(孔子说："君子不局限于一才一艺之用。")

Confucius said, "A virtuous man should not possess one skill only." (*The Analects*)

◎朴散则为器，圣人用之则为官长。(《老子·二十八章》)

（真朴的道分散则成为各种器物，圣人善于任使不同功用的"器"，就成为百官的首长。）

Dao disperses and gives birth to tangible objects, and sages who are good at making use of objects of different functions become natural leaders of all officials. (*Laozi*)

qiánshì-bùwàng, hòushìzhīshī 前事不忘，后事之师

Past Experience, If Not Forgotten, Is a Guide for the Future.

过去的事情不能忘记，它可作为以后行事的借鉴。"前事"即过去的事，亦即历史；"后事"即后来的事，亦即现在和未来；"师"即效法、借鉴。其深层含义在于提醒人们要从历史中吸取经验教训，以此作为后来的参照或借鉴。中国古代注重修史，史学空前发达，为的就是总结前代治国理政的成败得失，叙述历史人物特别是帝王与执政官员个人言行的是非善恶，对当代和后世起到警示与借鉴的作用。

This concept is meant to remind people of the need to learn from past experience and make it a guide for the future. In ancient China great importance was attached to writing history and thus historiography experienced great progress. It was so designed as to review the successes and failures of previous dynasties and recount the good and evil in historical figures, especially sovereigns and officials, in order to provide a warning or a guide for the future.

引例 Citations：

◎ 臣观成事，闻往古，天下之美同，臣主之权均之能美，未之有也。前事之不忘，后事之师。(《战国策·赵策一》)

（我考察古往今来发生的事情，发现普天之下美的东西总是相同的，但臣下与君主权势均等而能和美相处的，这种事情从来也没出现过。过去的事情不能忘记，它可作为以后行事的借鉴。）

In observing past events and learning of ancient times, I have found that the good things in the world are always the same, but it has never occurred that when a sovereign and his officials have had equal power, they can still live harmoniously. We should not forget past experience, but instead use it as a guide for the future. (*Strategies of the Warring States*)

◎ 又闻前事为后事之师，古人为今人之则，据其年代，虽则不同，量彼是非，必然无异。(赵普《上太宗请班师》)

（又听说从前发生的事情是后人行事的借鉴，古人的言行可作为今人言行的准则，虽然事情发生的年代有不同，但考察其蕴含的是非道理一定不会有差异。）

I have heard that past events are a guide to future events and that the words and actions of ancient people provide models for people of the present age. Even though time has changed, they are not off the mark in providing criteria for right and wrong. (Zhao Pu: Memorial Urging Emperor Taizong to Withdraw Troops)

qiú fàngxīn 求放心

Search for the Lost Heart

寻求、找回丧失的本心。"求放心"是孟子（前372？—前289）所提出的一种道德修养方法。孟子认为，每个人天生都具有善心，也即是"四端"，它是每个人都有的天赋德性，是人之为善的根源。但在人的成长过程中，受到外在事物与环境的影响，固有的善心可能会被削弱和遮蔽，从而出现违背道德的言行。因此在个人的道德修养中，需要努力发现并找回自己所固有的善心。

To search for and retrieve one's lost heart is a way to cultivate one's morality propounded by Mencius (372?-289 BC). In his view everyone was born with a benevolent heart, which meant the "four initiators" of benevolence, righteousness, rites and social norms, and wisdom. These are virtues conferred by Heaven and the sources of human kindness. However, people may be influenced by external factors or the environment when growing up. In that case, their innate goodness may be weakened or obscured and hence they may act or speak in contrary to moral principles. Therefore, when cultivating one's moral character, one must find and recover one's innate good heart.

引例 Citation：

◎人有鸡犬放，则知求之；有放心，而不知求。学问之道无他，求其放心而已矣。(《孟子·告子上》)

（人丢失了所养的鸡、犬，则知道去寻找；丢失了本心，却不知道寻找。学问之道没有别的，就是要寻求、找回丢失的本心而已。）

One surely knows to look for the chicken or dog and bring them back when he loses them. However, one may not know to look for his heart when he loses it. The way of learning is no other than searching for one's lost heart. (*Mencius*)

qǔ 曲

Qu (Melody)

　　曲是继诗、词之后兴起的一种文学体式，一般指宋金以来的北曲（音乐多用北方曲调，演唱和念白用北方音）和南曲（音乐多用南方曲调，演唱和念白用南方音）。因鼎盛于元代，故又称为元曲。"曲"与词的体制相近，但句法较词灵活，多用口语，用韵也接近口语。曲大致分为两种类型：一种是进入杂剧、传奇的唱词，属于戏曲（也称剧曲）；另一种是散曲，和诗词一样，可抒情、写景、叙事，能演唱，但没有念白和关于人物动作、表情等的提示语，又称为"清曲"。不过，总体上说，古代戏曲的成就和影响要大大超过散曲，而元代又是中国戏曲史上的黄金时代，当时有姓名记载的戏曲作家就有八十余人。关汉卿、马致远（1251？—1321后）、白朴（1226—1306后）、郑光祖（？—1324前）四位戏曲作家，代表了元代不同时期、不同流派的戏曲创作成就，因此后人称他们为"元曲四大家"。元曲在思想内容和艺术成就两方面都体现了独有的特色，和唐诗、宋词、明清小说一样，成为中国文学史上一座重要的里程碑。

Qu (曲) is a literary form that came into being later than poetry and *ci* (词). It generally refers to the northern- and southern-style melodies created in the Song and Jin dynasties. Northern melodies were composed mostly with tunes in northern China and performed in northern dialect, while southern melodies had southern tunes and southern dialect. Since *qu* reached its peak in the Yuan Dynasty, it is generally known as Yuan *qu* or Yuan opera. *Qu* is similar to *ci* in form but is more flexible in sentence structure, and colloquial language is used. There are two main types of *qu*: one is northern *zaju* (杂剧) opera and southern *chuanqi* (传奇) opera; such *qu* is known as *xiqu* (戏曲) or *juqu* (剧曲). The other type is *sanqu* (散曲) or lyric songs, also known as *qingqu* (清曲). As with other forms of poetry, *sanqu* describes a scene, a sentiment or an event and can be sung, but it has no spoken parts or instructions for performers' movements and expressions. Generally speaking, the old-style opera is much more accomplished and influential than *sanqu*. The Yuan period was a golden age in the development of Chinese opera. There are more than 80 known playwrights from that time. Guan Hanqing, Ma Zhiyuan (1251?-1321?), Bai Pu (1226-1306?), and Zheng Guangzu (?- 1324?) represent different styles from different stages of the Yuan opera, and they are recognized as the four leading Yuan opera writers. Yuan opera has distinctive plots and artistic appeal. Together with Tang and Song poetry and Ming and Qing fiction, it marks an important milestone in the historical development of Chinese literature.

引例 Citation：

◎世称曲手，必曰关、郑、白、马。（王骥德《曲律·杂论》）

（世人称元代戏曲高手，一定推关汉卿、郑光祖、白朴、马致远四人。）

When it comes to leading opera writers of the Yuan Dynasty, Guan Hanqing, Zheng Guangzu, Bai Pu, and Ma Zhiyuan come to mind. (Wang Jide: *On the Melody and Writing of Chinese Operas*)

rénzhě-àirén 仁者爱人

A Benevolent Person Loves Others.

仁者对他人充满仁爱之心。"仁者"即有仁德的人,是有大智大勇、德行完满、关爱他人、有人格魅力和感召力的人。"仁"在孔子(前551—前479)那里是最高的道德范畴和境界,以"爱人"为基本规定,意思是"仁"从孝父母、敬兄长开始,进而关爱家族其他成员,进而扩大至全天下的人。孟子(前372?—前289)将其提炼为思想命题,并应用于治国理政,提出君子由亲爱亲人而仁爱百姓,由仁爱百姓而爱惜万物。在儒家看来,人虽然有差等,但仁爱却是普遍的。它是构建和谐、友善社会的基础和目标。

The benevolent person has a loving heart. *Renzhe* (仁者) refers to benevolent and virtuous people or people with loving hearts, who have tremendous courage, wisdom, perfect moral character, charm, and charisma, and who love and care about others. Confucianism holds *ren* (仁) as the highest moral value. The basic meaning of *ren* is loving others, and to love others, one should first show filial piety to one's parents and respect one's elder brothers, and then extend love and care to other family members, and eventually to everyone else in the world. Mencius (372?-289 BC) synthesized and upgraded this notion into a theory to be applied to the governance of a country. He proposed that a person of virtue should love and care about first his loved ones, then other people, and finally everything on earth. Confucianism believed that love could be extended to people in a certain order, but that benevolence has general value, which is both the foundation and the goal of building a harmonious and good-will society.

引例 Citations:

◎仁者爱人，有礼者敬人。爱人者，人恒爱之；敬人者，人恒敬之。(《孟子·离娄下》)

(仁者爱别人，有礼节的人尊敬别人。爱别人的人，别人总也爱他；尊敬别人的人，别人总也尊敬他。)

Benevolent people care for others, and courteous people show respect for others. Those who care about others can always be cared about by others; those who show respect for others will always be respected by others. (*Mencius*)

◎亲亲而仁民，仁民而爱物。(《孟子·尽心上》)

(君子亲爱亲人，因而仁爱百姓；仁爱百姓，因而爱惜万物。)

Men of virtue love and care for their loved ones, they are therefore kind to other people. When they are kind to people, they treasure everything on earth. (*Mencius*)

sānbiǎo 三表

Three Standards

衡量言论正确与否的三条标准。表：标准，准则。墨子（前468？—前376）主张通过言论判断是非，应以"三表"作为标准：其一，以历史上圣王成功的治理经验作为标准。其二，以民众的实际经验作为标准。其三，以言论应用的实践效果是否有利于国家、人民作为标准。墨子以"三表"为依据建立自己的学说，并以此考量、批评其他学派的主张。

The term means the three standards used to measure the truth of an assertion.

The Chinese character *biao* (表) in this term means standard or norm. Mozi (468?-376 BC) believed in judging right or wrong by following the three standards. The first one was the successful way in which the ancient sage kings had ruled. The second one was the actual experience of the people. The third one was whether one's words and deeds actually served the interests of the state and people. Mozi established his school of thought on the basis of the three standards and used them to evaluate and criticize the doctrines of other schools.

引例 Citation：

◎ ［言］必立仪，言而毋仪，譬犹运钧之上而立朝夕者也，是非利害之辨，不可得而明知也，故言必有三表。(《墨子·非命上》)

（[言论]必须确定标准，言论没有标准，就如同在一直旋转的制陶转轮上测定早晚的时刻，是非利害的分辨不可能得到明确的答案，因此言论[正确与否]必须有三个标准。）

To make assertions one must establish a standard of judgment. Speaking without a standard is analogous to trying to determine the time of sunrise and sunset on a revolving potter's wheel. Distinctions of right and wrong, benefit and harm, cannot be clearly derived. Therefore, we must have the three standards. (*Mozi*)

sāncái 三才

Three Elements

"三才"指天、地、人。《易传》在解释《易》的卦象时提出了"三才"之说。在由"—"（阳爻）、"--"（阴爻）六画所组成的一卦中，处于下位的初爻（一爻）、二爻象征地，中间的三爻、四爻象征生活在天地之间的人，上位的五爻、六爻象征天。六画统一于一卦之中，也即象征着天、地、人是一个整体。三者遵循着共通的法则，但在各自的领域中法则的具体表现有所不同。

The three elements refer to heaven, earth, and man. When explaining the trigrams, *Commentary on The Book of Changes* proposes the idea of the "three elements." In a trigram which consists of six undivided and divided lines, the first and second lines at the bottom represent earth, the third and fourth lines in the center represent man who lives between earth and heaven, and the fifth and sixth lines at the upper part represent heaven. Collectively, the six lines united in one diagram signify the whole of heaven, earth, and man. The three elements share the same rules but have different manifestations of rules in their each field.

引例 Citations：

◎是以立天之道曰阴与阳，立地之道曰柔与刚，立人之道曰仁与义。兼三才而两之，故《易》六画而成卦。(《周易·说卦》)
（所以确立天的法则为阴与阳，确立地的法则为柔与刚，确立人世的法则为仁与义。兼有象征天地人的卦画而两画一组，因此《周易》是六画构成一卦。）

So the law of heaven is governed by yin and yang; the law of earth is governed by softness and hardness; and the law of man is governed by benevolence and righteousness. Each trigram, described in *The Book of Changes*, consists of six lines with each two being a unit representing heaven, earth and man. (*The Book of Changes*)

◎《易》一物而三才备：阴阳气也，而谓之天；刚柔质也，而谓之地；仁义德也，而谓之人。（张载《横渠易说》卷三）

（《周易》一卦而具备三才：具备阴阳之气的而称之为天，具备刚柔质性的而称之为地，具备仁义品德的而称之为人。）

Each trigram in *The Book of Changes* consists of three elements: the *qi* of yin and yang representing heaven, the quality of softness and hardness representing earth, and the virtue of benevolence and righteousness representing man. (Zhang Zai: *Zhang Zai's Explanation of The Book of Changes*)

sānsī'érxíng 三思而行

Think Carefully Before Taking Action

指经过多次思考以后再去施行（"三"原指三次，但在古书中又常表示"多"）。是一种过于谨慎的处事态度。适度的思考是正当言行的前提，但如果思虑过于谨慎，则容易心生顾虑、犹豫，使对私利的关切影响对道义的遵守。《论语》记述春秋鲁大夫季文子"三思而后行"，孔子（前551—前479）认为，季文子思考两次即可，不必三思。后人在使用"三思而行"一词时，或淡化其过度谨慎之义，仅用以劝诫谨慎行事，强调在言语行事之前应反复周详地思考，从而做出符合日用伦常之道的选择。

The term refers to taking action after having reflected several times (The number three is often used in ancient literature to mean several or many times). This is a kind of attitude handling things too cautiously. An appropriate measure of reflection is a prerequisite for proper speech and action, but if one becomes too cautious, then hesitation and doubt easily arise in the mind, affecting the observance of morality in the face of personal gain. *The Analects* records that Ji Wenzi, a senior official of the State of Lu in the Spring and Autumn Period, "acted having reflected thrice." Confucius (551-479 BC) thought that it would suffice if Ji reflected twice and that there was no need to reflect three times. When people later used the expression "thinking thrice before acting," they weakened the meaning of being too cautious, and just used it to urge caution when acting. They stressed that one should carefully reflect before speaking or acting so as to be in conformity with accepted moral standards.

引例 Citation：

◎季文子三思而后行。子闻之，曰："再，斯可矣。"(《论语·公冶长》)

(季文子三思之后才去行事。孔子听闻后说："思考两次就可以了。")

Ji Wenzi acted after having reflected thrice. When Confucius heard it, he remarked, "Twice is sufficient." (*The Analects*)

shèndú 慎独

Shendu (Ethical Self-cultivation)

儒家提出的一种道德修养方法。"慎独"有两种不同含义：其一，将"独"理解为闲居独处。人们在独处时，没有他人的监督，最容易放纵行事。"慎独"即要求在独处时谨慎对待自己的行为，自觉遵守道德、礼法的要求。其二，将"独"理解为内心的真实状态。人们可以在言行上表现出符合道德、礼法的要求，但心中却没有对道德、礼法的认同与追求。"慎独"则要求在心上做工夫，使内心与道德、礼法所要求的言行相符。

A kind of ethical self-cultivation advanced by the Confucian school of thought, the term has two different meanings. First, *du* (独) is understood as at leisure and alone. When people are alone, without someone else's supervision, they easily act in an undisciplined and immoral way. *Shendu* (慎独) requires being careful with one's conduct when being alone, consciously following morality and the requirements of etiquette. Second, *du* is understood as an inner true state. People may in their words and actions manifest what is in accord with morality and the requirements of etiquette, but in their heart they do not accept or pursue any morality or etiquette. *Shendu* requires that one makes efforts in one's heart, so that one's inner world is in agreement with the words and actions required by morality and etiquette.

引例 Citations：

◎是故君子戒慎乎其所不睹，恐惧乎其所不闻。莫见（xiàn）乎隐，莫显乎微，故君子慎其独也。(《礼记·中庸》)
（因此君子在没有人看见时也是谨慎的，在没有人听到时也是有所恐惧的。没有比隐蔽的地方更容易表现的了，没有比隐微的地方更容易显明的了，因此君子应"慎独"。）

A man of virtue is cautious when he is not being watched by others and apprehensive when what he says is not being heard. There is nothing more visible than in what is secret, and nothing more obvious than in what is vague and minute. Therefore, a man of virtue is watchful when he is at leisure and alone. (*The Book of Rites*)

◎此谓诚于中，形于外，故君子必慎其独也。(《礼记·大学》)
（这是说实存于内心的东西，会表现在外，因此君子必须"慎独"。）

This means what one truly believes in his heart and mind will find expression in the open. That is why a man of virtue must be cautious when he is at leisure and alone. (*The Book of Rites*)

shènsī-míngbiàn 慎思明辨

Careful Reflection and Clear Discrimination

谨慎周密地思考，清晰明确地分辨。古人认为，人的成长包括五个阶段：博学（广博地学习），即收集信息，吸取知识；审问（详尽地追问），即提出问题，解除疑惑；慎思（谨慎周密地思考），即消化整理，融会贯通；明辨（清晰明确地分辨），即形成概念，择定结果；笃行（切实地实行），即将认知付诸实践，形成品格。这五个阶段大致可约为学习、思考、实践三个方面。"慎思明辨"就是思考，是由学习到实践的中间阶段。也就是说，学习与思考、学习与实践是相辅相成的；而思考则是学习的深入和提升，是实践的前导，是从学习到实践转化的关键所在。

It was thought in ancient China that a person matured through five stages: broad study for collecting information and acquiring knowledge, close examination for identifying problems and resolving doubts, careful reflection for absorbing and mastering knowledge, clear discrimination for developing concepts and reaching conclusions, and earnest practice for putting knowledge into practice and developing character. These stages can be roughly divided into three areas: learning, reflection, and practice. "Careful reflection and clear discrimination" describes the stage of reflection between learning and practice. It can also be said that study and reflection on the one hand and study and practice on the other complement each other, while reflection is a deepening and heightening of learning, a prerequisite for practice, and a key link between learning and practice.

引例 Citation：

◎博学之，审问之，慎思之，明辨之，笃行之。(《礼记·中庸》)
（广泛地学习，详尽地追问，谨慎周密地思考，清晰明确地判别，切实地践行。）

Learn broadly, examine closely, reflect carefully, discriminate clearly, and practice earnestly. (*The Book of Rites*)

shīzhí-wéizhuàng 师直为壮

Troops Will Be Powerful When Fighting a Just Cause.

用兵有正当的理由，士气就旺盛，富有战斗力。"师"泛指军队，在此指出兵、进军征伐；"直"即正，指名义、理由正当；"壮"即壮盛，有力量。中华民族自古不轻言战争，而是注重战争的正义性，并且相信为正义而战的军队一定斗志旺盛，所向无敌。

This term suggests that when there is a good cause to use military force, the troops will be high in morale and valiant in fighting. The word *shi* (师) here is a general term for all military forces and operations. The word *zhi* (直) means a just cause. The word *zhuang* (壮) means powerful troops. The Chinese nation has always been wary of waging wars, believing that a war should be fought only for a just cause and that an army fighting for such a cause will have high morale and win the war.

引例 Citation：

◎师直为壮，曲为老，岂在久乎？（《左传·僖公二十八年》）
（出兵作战，理由正当就会气壮，理由不正当就会气衰，哪里因军队长久在外呢？）

In fighting a just war, the troops will have high morale and be powerful, while they suffer from poor morale when the cause is unjust. Morale has nothing to do with how long an army is deployed at the front. (*Zuo's Commentary on The Spring and Autumn Annals*)

shī 诗

Shi (Poetry)

中国古代文学的主要体式，也是中国古代最早产生的文学体式。它按照一定的节奏、韵律、字数和句式要求，用凝练的语言、丰富的想象反映社会生活、表达思想情感。"诗"与"文"是中国古代文学的主要形态，古人所说的"诗"主要分古体诗和近体诗，一般不包括唐以后出现的词曲。古体诗也叫古风，是近体诗产生前除楚辞体之外的各种诗体的通称，其格律比较自由，不拘对仗、平仄，押韵较宽，篇幅长短不限，句子有四言、五言、六言、七言、杂言；近体诗也叫格律诗，它的字数、押韵、平仄、对仗都有严格的规定，有五绝、七绝、五律、七律、排律等。诗与词曲的区别是：诗不配乐，词曲可配乐歌唱。在中国，诗已有两千多年的历史，古人认为诗能够连通人与自然、表达志向、抒发情性，集中体现了中国文学艺术的精神特质与审美追求，这与西方将诗看作文学的门类很不相同。在中国古代，儒家思想对诗的创作有重要指导作用，而道家与佛教思想对于诗的意境理论影响深远。因中国最早的诗集是《诗经》，所以后世也用"诗"专指《诗经》。

Shi (诗) is a major genre of ancient Chinese literature, the earliest literary form that emerged in China. Observing the requirements of a certain rhythm, rules of rhyming, number of characters, and type of verses, and using concise language and rich imagination, it reflects social life and conveys thoughts and emotions. *Shi* and *wen* (文 essay) are two principal forms of ancient Chinese literature. *Shi*, as referred to by the ancient Chinese, consists of the older type of poetry and the latter type of poetry. It generally does not include *ci* (词 lyric) and *qu* (曲 melody), which appeared as literary genres after the Tang Dynasty. The older type of *shi* is also called *gufeng* (古风), meaning ancient style, which is a general appellation for all kinds of poetic forms produced prior to the latter type of *shi*, except the style employed in *Odes of Chu*. With relatively few restrictions in rules and forms, *shi* is not constrained by any antithetical arrangement or a fixed tone pattern, and its rhyme is fairly free. In addition, the length of a piece is not limited. A verse may have four, six, seven, or a mixed number of Chinese characters. The latter type of *shi* is also called *gelüshi* (格律诗), meaning poetry with fixed patterns. Its number of characters, rhyming, tone pattern, and antithetical arrangement are all strictly fixed. A poem of this type may contain four lines (known as *jue* 绝), each with five or seven characters, or eight lines (known as *lü* 律), each with five or seven characters. Occasionally, it is much longer than normal, expanding to one and a half dozen lines, which is referred to as *pailü* (排律). The difference between *shi*, and *ci* and *qu* is that the former is not set to music, while the latter may be set to music and sung. *Shi* has existed as a literary form for more than 2,000 years in China. Ancient Chinese used *shi* to connect humans with nature, voice aspirations, and give expression to emotions. It embodied the spirit and aesthetic pursuits of literature and art in ancient China, which is very different from the West, which only sees poetry as a category of literature. In ancient China, Confucian thought played an important guiding role in poetic creation, while Daoist and Buddhist thoughts had a profound influence on the theory of poetry's artistic conception. Since *The Book of Songs* was China's earliest collection of poems, later generations also used *shi* to refer to *The Book of Songs* in particular.

引例 Citations：

◎诗言志，歌永言，声依永，律和声。(《尚书·舜典》)
(诗是表达内心志向的，歌是用语言来吟唱的。五音（宫、商、角、徵、羽）的高低变化要随吟唱而定，音律则要与五音谐和。)

Poems express aspirations deep in one's heart, whereas songs are verses for chanting. Undulation of tunes of five notes depends on chanting, and meter and melody must be in harmony with the five notes. (*The Book of History*)

◎诗，言其志也；歌，咏其声也；舞，动其容也。三者本于心，然后乐器从之。(《礼记·乐记》)
(诗，用语言表达人的志向；歌，用吟唱表达内心的想法；舞，是将内心的想法呈现于形体的各种舞姿。这三者都发自内心，之后才以乐器演奏加以配合。)

Shi expresses aspirations through written words, whereas songs do so via chanting. Dancing is a sequence of body movements to project one's emotions. All these three forms of art come forth from the heart, accompanied by musical performance. (*The Book of Rites*)

◎气之动物，物之感人，故摇荡性情，形诸舞咏。照烛三才，晖丽万有，灵祇（qí）待之以致飨，幽微藉之以昭告。动天地，感鬼神，莫近于诗。(钟嵘《诗品》卷上)

（四季的气候引起景物变化，景物变化感发人的内心，引起人的性情起伏跌宕，并通过舞蹈、吟咏表现出来。它辉映着天、地、人，让万物亮丽生辉，天上的神祇依赖它接受享祀，幽冥的神灵也通过它明告世人。而感动天地、鬼神的，没有比诗更接近的了。）

The four seasons bring changes in scenery, which in turn stir one's emotions. One gives expression to such emotions through dancing and chanting. Poetry thus illuminates heaven, earth and humans, making everything clear and bright. The gods in heaven rely on it to receive sacrificial rituals and the spirits in the nether world use it to communicate with the world. Among those which move heaven, earth and the spirits, nothing comes near poetry! (Zhong Rong: *The Critique of Poetry*)

shòurényǐyú 授人以渔

Teaching How to Fish

把捕鱼的方法传授给别人。授：给予，传授。渔：捕鱼。原话是"授人以鱼，不如授人以渔"，意思是，把鱼给予别人，不如把捕鱼的方法传授给他。其喻义为：与其直接给人某种东西，不如教人学会如何获得它的方法，使他能够通过自身的努力获得这种东西。其蕴含的道理主要有：其一，在目标已定的情况下，达到目标的方法更重要；其二，帮助他人及管理他人的长远有效的方法是使人自立。

This term expresses the idea that giving away a fish is not as good as teaching one how to fish. The meaning is that rather than giving something away it is better to teach the method of obtaining it so that people can get what they need through their own efforts. It implies that once an objective is established, the method of achieving it becomes most important, and that the effective way of helping and managing people in the long term is to encourage them to be self-supporting.

引例 Citation:

◎授人以鱼，只供一餐；授人以渔，可享一生。（民间谚语）
（给人鱼吃，只能供他一顿；教人捕鱼，可使他受用终身。）

To give people a fish and you only provide them with one meal; to teach them to fish and they can benefit throughout their lives. (Chinese proverb)

shù 恕

Being Considerate / Forgiveness

"恕"的基本含义是推己及人、将心比心。人可以根据自身对于厌恶之事的感受去理解、体贴他人的意愿。基于这种对他人的理解，人应避免将自己厌恶之事强加于他人，这即是"恕"。在执法者或受伤害者面对有过之人的情境中，"恕"被引申为宽恕、赦免之义。

The basic meaning of the term is to put oneself in another person's position and have empathy, and to reflect what one would do in the same kind of situation. Starting out from their own likes and dislikes, people can understand and show considerations for the wishes of others, and on the basis of such understanding, people should refrain from imposing their own likes and dislikes on others. This is what it means to be considerate. To those enforcing the law and to the victims of wrongdoing, the meaning of the term extended to mean forgiveness or pardon.

引例 Citations：

◎子贡问曰："有一言而可以终身行之者乎？"子曰："其恕乎！己所不欲，勿施于人。"（《论语·卫灵公》）

（子贡问道："有没有一句教导可以让我终身奉行呢？"孔子说："那就是恕吧！自己不想要的，不要施加于他人。"）

Zigong asked, "Is there any teaching that can serve as a lasting principle for conduct in one's whole life?" Confucius replied, "Surely that is to be considerate! Do not do to others what you do not want others to do to you." (*The Analects*)

◎推己之谓恕。（朱熹《论语集注》卷二）

（以自己的感受去理解、体贴他人就是恕。）

To extend one's mind to understand others is called "being considerate." (Zhu Xi: *The Analects Variorum*)

sìhǎi zhī nèi jiē xiōngdì 四海之内皆兄弟

All the People Within the Four Seas Are Brothers.

全天下的人都亲如兄弟。也说"四海皆兄弟"。"四海"即东海、西海、南海、北海。古人认为天圆地方，中国居陆地中间，陆地四周由四海环绕。"四海之内"指当时已知的人类生活空间，犹言"天下"，意指全国或全世界。它昭示了中国人兼济天下的博大胸怀、仁爱友善的人文精神。

This saying means that all the people in the world are as close as brothers. The Four Seas are the East, West, South, and North seas. The ancient Chinese believed that heaven was round and the earth was square, with China in the middle of the earth, which was surrounded on all four sides by the Four Seas. "Within the Four Seas" refers to the world inhabited by humans, which was also called "all under heaven," referring to the whole country or the whole world. This saying shows the inclusive and broad mind of the Chinese and their compassion, love and friendship towards other human beings.

引例 Citation：

◎君子敬而无失，与人恭而有礼，四海之内皆兄弟也。(《论语·颜渊》)
（君子做事认真而不出差错，待人谦恭而合于礼，那么天下所有的人都是他的兄弟。）

A man of virtue always does things conscientiously without making any mistakes and treats people respectfully and appropriately. Then all within the Four Seas will be his brothers. (*The Analects*)

tàixū 太虚

Taixu (Great Void)

虚空的境地或事物虚空的状态。张载（1020—1077）对"太虚"的含义进行了深入的阐发。他认为，天地万物都是由"气"构成的。而"太虚"是"气"的一种无形而虚静的状态。这一状态是"气"的本然状态。"太虚"凝聚而为"气"，"气"消散而复归于"太虚"。"太虚"只是无法被人感知，并不是绝对的空虚无有。"太虚"的属性通过"气"而赋予天地万物。

Taixu (太虚) refers to a state of void in both space and things. Zhang Zai (1020-1077), a thinker in the Song Dynasty, elaborated on the meaning of *taixu*, or great void. He believed that all things in heaven and on earth were made up of *qi* (气), and that *taixu* was its natural state, which was formless and motionless. When *taixu* coalesced, it turned into *qi*; when *qi* dissipated, it became *taixu*. Though *taixu* could not be felt by humans, it was not absolute emptiness and nothingness. *Taixu* gave life to all things in heaven and on earth by means of *qi*.

引例 Citations：

◎是以不过乎昆仑，不游乎太虚。(《庄子·知北游》)
(因此不能越过昆仑之山，不能巡游于太虚之中。)

And so, they will not be able to go beyond Mount Kunlun, nor can they wander in the great void. (*Zhuangzi*)

◎太虚无形，气之本体，其聚其散，变化之客形尔。(张载《正蒙·太和》)
(太虚是无形的，是气的本来状态，气或聚或散，不过是太虚变化的暂时形态罢了。)

Taixu is formless; it is the original state of *qi*. Whether *qi* coalesces or dissipates, it is just a temporary form of *taixu*, or great void. (Zhang Zai: *Enlightenment Through Confucian Teachings*)

tiāndào 天道

Way of Heaven

天地万物的存在与变化所遵循的基本法则（与"人道"相对）。古人对"天道"的理解并不相同：其一，认为"天道"尤其是与日月星辰运行有关的天象暗示或决定着人事的吉凶成败。古代有专门的职官负责通过对天象的观察来推知人事。其二，认为"天道"是人的道德与人伦秩序的根源或依据。人的言行以及人伦秩序应该效法"天道"，或者通过体认、发挥"天"所赋予的心性来通达"天道"。其三，认为"天道"与人世的道德、秩序乃至人事祸福之间都没有必然的关联。

The way of heaven refers to the basic rule governing the existence and changes of all things between heaven and earth (as opposed to the "way of man"). Ancient Chinese interpreted the "way of heaven" in different ways. First, some believed that "the way of heaven," especially the celestial phenomena relating to the movements of the sun, the moon, and the stars, foretell or dictate the success or failure of human affairs. In ancient times, designated officials predicted human affairs through observing celestial phenomena. Second, some believed that "the way of heaven" was the source or the basis of man's moral conduct and of orderly human relations. One should comply with "the way of heaven," in both words and deeds, so should human relations; and people should recognize and develop the moral nature bestowed upon by heaven so as to gain access to "the way of heaven." Third, still others thought that there were no particular correlations between "the way of heaven" on the one hand, and moral conduct in the human world, human relations, as well as misfortune and fortune in human affairs on the other.

引例 Citations：

◎是以立天之道曰阴与阳，立地之道曰柔与刚，立人之道曰仁与义。(《周易·说卦》)

（所以确立天的法则为阴与阳，确立地的法则为柔与刚，确立人世的法则为仁与义。）

The laws governing the ways of heaven are yin and yang, those governing the ways of earth are gentleness and firmness, and those governing the ways of human society are benevolence and righteousness. (*The Book of Changes*)

◎诚者，天之道也；诚之者，人之道也。(《礼记·中庸》)

("诚"，是天的法则；达到"诚"，是人的修养的路径。)

Integrity is what the way of nature requires; acting with integrity is the way to achieve self-refinement. (*The Book of Rites*)

◎天道远，人道迩。(《左传·昭公十八年》)

(天之道遥远，人事之道切近。)

The way of heaven is far away; the way of man is near. (*Zuo's Commentary on The Spring and Autumn Annals*)

tiānlǐ 天理

Natural Law / Principles of Heaven

天地万物与人类社会所遵循的普遍法则。宋明儒者认为，"天"的本质意义就是"天理"，并将"天理"作为具有终极意义的最高范畴。"天理"是事物的本体或本原，决定着人与事物的本性，是自然法则与人伦道德的依据。"天理"超越于有形的具体事物，但又包含在每一个具体事物之中。在人性之中，"天理"表现为人天生所禀受的至善之性，常与"人欲"相对。

The term means the universal law observed by all things in heaven and on earth as well as by human society. Confucian scholars in the Song and Ming dynasties held that the essence of heaven was natural law, and they regarded natural law as the realm of ultimate significance. Natural law is the essence or the source of things, deciding the inherent nature of humans and things. It is the law of nature and the foundation of moral conduct in the human society. Natural law transcends visible, concrete things, but it also exists in each concrete thing. In terms of human nature, natural law expresses itself in the innate good nature one is bestowed upon by heaven, as opposed to "human desire."

引例 Citations：

◎万物皆只是一个天理。(《二程遗书》卷二上)
(万物都只是天理的具体呈现。)

All things are but manifestations of the natural law. (*Writings of the Cheng Brothers*)

◎性即天理，未有不善者也。(朱熹《孟子集注》卷十一)
(人性就是天理，没有不是善的。)

Human nature reflects the natural law, which is necessarily benign. (Zhu Xi: *Mencius Variorum*)

tiānmìng 天命

Mandate of Heaven

　　天的命令与赐予。"天命"主要包含三种不同含义：其一，指天对于人事的命令。命令的内容最初集中于王权的更替，即上天授命有德者征讨并取代失德之君，享有至高无上的权力和福禄。其二，指命运，具有不可抗拒之义，标志着人力的限度。其三，指天赋予人的禀性。《中庸》称"天命之谓性"。宋儒发挥这一思想，以"天命之性"指称人禀受于天的纯善的本性。

The term means order and bestowment from Heaven. "Mandate of heaven" mainly contains three different meanings. The first is the order of heaven over human affairs. Such order first of all focuses on a change of the supreme ruler's authority. Heaven empowers the virtuous to attack and replace a ruler who has lost his virtue, and thus enjoy the highest and unsurpassed power and benefits. Secondly, mandate of heaven means fate, which is irresistible and imposes limit on human power. Thirdly, the term indicates the natural disposition bestowed by heaven upon human being. According to *The Doctrine of the Mean*, "Mandate of heaven endows one with his nature." Song-dynasty Confucian scholars developed this idea, proposing that human nature was the "nature of mandate of heaven," that is, the inherent pure and good nature one receives from heaven.

引例 Citations：

◎天命靡常。(《诗经·大雅·文王》)
（上天的命令没有恒常不变的。）

Heaven-bestowed supreme power is not eternal. (*The Book of Songs*)

◎莫之为而为者天也，莫之致而至者命也。(《孟子·万章上》)
（没有人能做到却做到了，这是天意；没有人求它来它却来到了，这是命运。）

That which no man can do but is accomplished is the mandate of heaven. That which no man asks but comes is from fate. (*Mencius*)

tiānmìngzhīxìng 天命之性

Character Endowed by Heaven

　　天所赋予人的道德本性，又称"天地之性"（与"气质之性"相对）。先秦时期即有儒者提出人的道德本性源自于天。宋儒继承这一观念，提出了"天命之性"的概念，用以指称每个人都具有的禀受于天的道德本性。"天命之性"是纯善的，是人的道德行为的内在依据。但由于人性还受到其他因素的影响，"天命之性"可能会被遮蔽。

This term refers to the moral character endowed to a person by Heaven, also known as "characters endowed by Heaven and Earth," as opposed to the "character endowed by *qi*, or vital force." Some early pre-Qin Confucian scholars maintained that human moral characters originated from Heaven. Confucian scholars of the Song Dynasty, inheriting this concept, further propounded the notion of "characters endowed by Heaven," meaning that all people were endowed by Heaven with moral characters. "Characters endowed by Heaven" are purely good, providing the inner basis for a person's moral principle and conduct. However, as human characters are subject to other influences, "characters endowed by Heaven" can be obscured.

引例 Citations：

◎形而后有气质之性，善反之则天地之性存焉。(张载《正蒙·诚明》)
(事物凝聚成形以后就禀受了气质之性，善于复归本原则天地之性得以实现。)

Physical matters take up their shape which acquires the properties of *qi*, or vital force; if we are thus good at returning to it, then the nature endowed by Heaven and Earth will be preserved. (Zhang Zai: *Enlightenment Through Confucian Teachings*)

◎天命之性，指理言；率性之道，指人物所行言。(《朱子语类》卷六十二)
(天命之性，是就天理而言的；率性之道，是就人的行事而言的。)

Characters endowed by Heaven refer to heavenly laws; the way of following those characters refers to human conduct. (*Categorized Conversations of Master Zhu Xi*)

tiānxià-xīngwáng, pǐfū-yǒuzé 天下兴亡，匹夫有责

Survival of a Nation Is the Responsibility of Every Individual.

天下的兴盛与衰亡，即便是普通百姓也有义不容辞的责任。源于明末清初著名思想家顾炎武（1613—1682）所说"保天下者，匹夫之贱，与有责焉耳矣"。"天下"在古代多指天子统治或名义下的中国全部疆域，而顾炎武提出"天下"与"国"是完全不同的概念："国"仅代表帝王一家一姓，而"天下"所代表的则是整个中华民族及中华文明的统系。近代思想家梁启超（1873—1929）等继承了顾炎武的这一思想，并将其概括为"天下兴亡，匹夫有责"，使语意更为显豁、语势更为有力，后经许多政治家、思想家的引用，这句话最终成为中国家喻户晓的名言。近代以来，它对激发中国人的爱国主义精神，唤醒人们心系民族和国家安危并以天下为己任，产生了巨大影响。

The view that ordinary people also share responsibility for the fate of the country originated with the famous late Ming- and early Qing-dynasty thinker Gu Yanwu (1613-1682). He stated that the ruler and his officials were in charge of the state apparatus, but guarding all under heaven was the responsibility of every individual, no matter how lowly they may be. In pre-modern China, all under heaven referred to the whole territory of China ruled either directly or nominally by the Son of Heaven. By "state" Gu Yanwu, however, meant something entirely different: the state only refers to one imperial house, while "all under heaven" refers to the whole of the Chinese nation and Chinese civilization. The modern Chinese thinker Liang Qichao (1873-1929) built on this idea and put it in more general terms stating that "survival of a nation is the responsibility of every individual," turning it into a clearer and more forceful statement. It was subsequently quoted by so many statesmen and thinkers that it became a household phrase. Ever since, this saying has had tremendous influence in arousing the patriotic spirit among the people of China and making them assume responsibility for the fate of their country.

引例 Citations：

◎易姓改号，谓之亡国；仁义充塞，而至于率兽食人，人将相食，谓之亡天下……保国者，其君其臣、肉食者谋之；保天下者，匹夫之贱，与有责焉耳矣。(顾炎武《日知录》卷十三"正始")

（换姓改朝，叫做"亡国"；而仁义道德得不到发扬，以至于统治者率领野兽吃人，民众也相互残害，叫做"亡天下"。……保有国家，只是帝王大臣及达官贵人去谋划；而保有天下，即便是地位卑微的普通百姓，也有责任。）

When one dynasty is replaced by another, it means the state of the old dynasty perishes. When benevolence and righteousness are obstructed to the point that the powerful lead others to exploit people and people fight each other, it means all under heaven perishes… Safeguarding the state is the concern of rulers, ministers, and officials; while safeguarding all under heaven is the responsibility of every individual, no matter how lowly they may be. (Gu Yanwu: *Records of Daily Study*)

◎顾炎武之言曰：天下兴亡，匹夫之贱与有责焉。(麦孟华《论今日疆臣之责任》)

（顾炎武有句话说：天下兴亡，即使是地位卑微的普通百姓也有责任。）

Gu Yanwu said: Survival of a nation is the responsibility of every individual, no matter how lowly they may be. (Mai Menghua: The Responsibilities of Officials in Charge of Current Border Affairs)

◎今欲国耻之一洒(xǐ)，其在我辈之自新……夫我辈则多矣，欲尽人而自新，云胡可致？我勿问他人，问我而已。斯乃真顾亭林所谓"天下兴亡，匹夫有责"也。(梁启超《痛定罪言》三)

(现在要一洗国家蒙受的耻辱，关键在于我们这些人的自我更新……我们人数当然很多，若是要所有人都实现自我更新，怎么可能做到呢？不必问其他人能否做到，只问自己能否做到就可以了。这确实像顾炎武所说的"天下兴亡，匹夫有责"啊！)

The key to wiping out our country's humiliation lies in our self-renewal… We have a large population, so it is impossible for every individual to achieve such self-renewal. We should do it ourselves whether or not others can also do it. This is just like what Gu Yanwu once said, "Survival of a nation is the responsibility of every individual." (Llang Qichao: Painful Reflections on Current Affairs Despite Possible Incrimination)

tóngguī-shūtú 同归殊途

Arrive at the Same Destination via Different Routes / Rely on a Common Ontological Entity

虽然有着相同的目标，但所走的道路不同。语出《周易·系辞下》，大致包含两方面的含义：其一，指不同学派、不同人对于社会秩序、价值的理解虽然不同，主张的社会治理方法也有差异，但他们的目标是一致的，都是谋求社会的安定、繁荣。其二，指万事万物虽然呈现出不同的样态，但他们都归附或依赖于一个共同的本体。

This term means to reach the same goal through different routes. Coming from *The Book of Changes*, the term has two meanings. First, different schools of thought and different people have different understandings of social order and values, and the ways of governance they advocate also vary, but their goals are the same – stability and prosperity of society. Second, though things under heaven manifest themselves in different ways, they all belong or rely on a common ontological entity.

引例 Citations：

◎天下同归而殊途，一致而百虑。(《周易·系辞下》)

(天下之人有着相同的目标，但所走的道路不同；有着相同的道理，但有上百种不同的想法。)

All people under heaven have the same goal, though they take different routes; they cherish the same principles, but they hold different views. (*The Book of Changes*)

◎子曰"天下同归而殊途，一致而百虑"，一本万殊之谓也。(王夫之《周易外传》卷六)

(孔子说"天下同归而殊途，一致而百虑"，是说天下万物依赖于一个共同的本体[本体表现在不同的事物之中]。)

Confucius said, "Under heaven, people have the same goal but they go by different routes." This means that all things under heaven rely on the same ontological entity. (Wang Fuzhi: *Explanatory Notes to The Book of Changes*)

wēngù-zhīxīn 温故知新

Review the Old and Learn the New

温习旧有的知识并获得新的理解与体会。有时也指回顾历史，对当代有新的指导意义。"温"，温习；"故"，指旧的、已知的知识；"新"，指新的、未知的知识。前人对"温故知新"的理解主要有两种：其一，将"温故"与"知新"理解为并列的两方面，认为在"温故"的同时就逐步获得新知，"知新"在"温故"的过程中得以实现。其二，将"温故"理解为"知新"的前提与基础，认为没有"温故"，就不可能"知新"；"新"是"故"的进一步发展，并且摒弃了其中陈腐的旧见。"温故知新"在今天已经超出一般学习方法的意义，也是个体、企业、组织甚至一个国家自我成长的基本机理。其中包含新与旧、古与今、已知与未知、继承与创新的辩证思想。

This term means to review what has been learned and to gain new understanding and new insights. It also means to obtain guidance in the present moment by recalling the past. *Wen* (温) means to review; *gu* (故) means knowledge that has been acquired in the past; *xin* (新) means new and unexplored knowledge. Our predecessors had two main approaches to interpreting this term. According to one approach, reviewing the knowledge acquired in the past and understanding new knowledge should be understood as two actions taking place at the same time. In other words, one gains new knowledge in the course of reviewing the old. According to the other, reviewing the knowledge acquired in the past should be viewed as the basis and precondition for understanding new knowledge. Without reviewing, one would not be able to understand new knowledge. Furthermore, the new knowledge is a development of the old on the basis of rejecting stale and outdated ideas of the past. Today, what this term offers is more than a simple methodology for studying, but rather a fundamental mechanism for the development of an individual, an enterprise, an organization, or even a country. The term expresses a dialectical logic between the old and new, past and present, known and unknown, and inheritance and innovation.

引例 Citation:

◎温故而知新，可以为师矣。(《论语·为政》)

(温习旧有的知识，并获得新的理解与体会，这样就可以成为他人的老师了。)

Reviewing what you have acquired and learning anew, this way you can be a teacher for others. (*The Analects*)

wúyù-zégāng 无欲则刚

People with No Covetous Desires Stand Upright.

人没有非分的贪欲，就能做到刚正凛然。"欲"指各种私欲、贪欲；"刚"即刚正公道、正直有力。"无欲"并不是绝对禁止人们有"欲"，而是提倡克制自己的私欲、贪欲。"无欲则刚"讲的是立身处事尤其是执政做官的基本道理：一个人面对来自各方的种种诱惑，应该大公无私、端正品行、淡泊守志，不要有非分的贪图，这样就能一身正气，无所畏惧，就像高高的峭壁一样，挺立于天地之间，坚不可摧。

People with no covetous desires stand upright and maintain integrity. *Yu* (欲)

refers to all sorts of selfish and covetous desires. *Gang* (刚) means fairness, justice, integrity, and forcefulness. *Wuyu* (无欲) does not mean that people should not have any desires, but rather, people should not harbor any selfish or covetous desires. The term tells us a basic principle for people to follow in conducting themselves, and especially for officials in handling office affairs, that is, no temptations should ever sway anyone. One must always conduct oneself properly without seeking to gratify personal interests; one must always seek compliance without seeking fame or wealth; and one must never harbor any greed. This is the way for one to stand upright, firm, and fearless. Like towering cliffs, one may stand tall and indestructible.

引例 Citations：

◎子曰："吾未见刚者。"或对曰："申枨(chéng)。"子曰："枨也欲，焉得刚？"（《论语·公冶长》）

（孔子说："我没见过刚正的人。"有人回应说："申枨就是。"孔子说："申枨欲望太多，哪里能够刚正呢？"）

Confucius said, "I have never seen any person of rectitude." Someone responded, "Shen Cheng is such a person." Confucius said, "Shen Cheng has too many desires. How can he be of rectitude?" (*The Analects*)

◎海纳百川，有容乃大；壁立千仞，无欲则刚。（林则徐对联）

（大海广阔接纳无数江河，人有度量才能［像大海那样］有大成就；千仞崖壁巍然屹立，人没有贪欲就能［像山崖那样］刚正凛然。）

The vast ocean accepts hundreds of rivers emptying into it; people with a broad mind can achieve greatness. Thousands of cliffs stand tall and lofty; people with no covetous desires stand firm and upright. (A couplet composed by Lin Zexu)

xiāngfǎn-xiāngchéng 相反相成

Being both Opposite and Complementary

处于对立关系中的两个事物之间既相互排斥又相互成就、相互转化。一切事物都处于与他者的对立之中。对立双方具有相反的性质或意义，因而彼此间是相互排斥的，如有与无、长与短、高与下、善与恶、美与丑等。但同时，事物的性质或意义又是借由与之对立的事物而获得确立的，对立双方在一定条件下还可以相互转化。这一观念在先秦时期即已出现，在班固（32—92）《汉书·艺文志》中始被概括为"相反相成"。

This term refers to two things that are mutually opposite to but complementing each other and that they mutually transform between them. Everything is an antithesis to something else. Both antithetic sides are opposite to each other. Therefore there is mutual exclusion between them, such as *you* and *wu*, long and short, high and low, good and bad, and beautiful and ugly. On the other hand, the nature or the identity of a thing is established due to something antithetic to it. The two opposing sides can transform into each other under certain conditions. This concept emerged in the pre-Qin period. In *The History of the Han Dynasty* written by Ban Gu (32-92), the idea was first defined as "two things being both opposite and complementary."

引例 Citations：

◎ 天下皆知美之为美，斯恶已；皆知善之为善，斯不善已。故有无相生，难易相成，长短相形，高下相倾，音声相和，前后相随。(《老子·二章》)
（天下都知道美之所以为美，丑恶的观念也就产生了；都知道善之所以为善，不善的观念也就产生了。因此有和无相互生成，难和易相互成就，长和短相互形成，高和下相互包含，音和声相互调和，前和后相互随顺。）

People all know that ugliness exists as an antithesis of beauty and that evil exists as an antithesis of goodness. Likewise, *you* and *wu* produce each other; what is difficult and what is easy complement each other; long and short exist in contrast, so do high and low; tone and sound are in harmony with each other, and front and back exist because of each other. (*Laozi*)

◎仁之与义，敬之与和，相反而皆相成也。（《汉书·艺文志》）

（仁与义、敬与和，既相互排斥又相互成就。）

The relationship between benevolence and righteousness and between respect and harmony is one of mutual opposition and complementation. (*The History of the Han Dynasty*)

xiàng 象

Xiang (Semblance)

可见而不具有形体的物象或图形。"象"大致包含四种不同的含义：其一，指"道"的某种显现形态。老子将"道"描述为"无物之象"，也称为"大象"。其二，指事物的某种显现形态。"象"的具体化或固定化程度要低于有形之物。常指"天象"，即日月星辰的运行、风雷云雨的施降。"天象"与"地形"相对。其三，指人的气象，即人的精神、意志在言行、姿态上的显现。其四，指象征或模拟天地万物的图形。古人创造了多种"象"的系统，并通过对"象"的观察与解释，来阐发自然与社会的运行变化及其法则。其中《周易》的卦象系统影响最为广远。

Xiang (象) refers to a visible but formless image or figure. It approximately has four different meanings. First, it refers to a manifest shape of Dao. Laozi described Dao as "a semblance of the unsubstantial," also called "the great semblance." Second, it indicates a manifest shape of objects. *Xiang* is less concrete or fixed than an object with a shape. It often means celestial phenomena, namely, the movements of the sun, the moon, and the stars, and the occurrence of wind, thunder, clouds, and rain. Celestial phenomena are relative to earthly shapes. Third, it refers to human temperament, namely, the human spirit and mind, manifested in words, deeds, and attitude. Fourth, it refers to figures symbolizing or imitating all things in heaven and on earth. Ancient Chinese created many kinds of systems of *xiang*, through the observation and interpretation of which they elucidated the changes in the movements of nature and of society, and also their laws. Among them, the system of the hexagrams and figures of *The Book of Changes* is the most influential.

引例 Citations：

◎其上不皦（jiǎo），在下不昧。绳（mǐn）绳不可名，复归于无物。是谓无状之状，无物之象，是谓惚恍。(《老子·十四章》)

（道在上而不明晰，在下也不晦暗。绵绵不绝而不能名状，返回到无物的状态。这可称作是没有形状的形状，不成物体的形象，称为"恍惚"。）

Above, Dao is not manifest, while lower down it is not obscure. It is ceaseless but cannot be described, and it then turns to nothingness. This is called the shape of the shapeless, and the semblance of the unsubstantial. Such a state is called intangible existence. (*Laozi*)

◎在天成象，在地成形，变化见矣。(《周易·系辞上》)

（在天空显现为象，在大地显现为形，在天地的形象之中显现出了事物的变化。）

In the heaven are phenomena, and on the earth are forms. Their movement demonstrates changes of things. (*The Book of Changes*)

◎圣人有以见天下之赜(zé)，而拟诸其形容，象其物宜，是故谓之象。(《周易·系辞上》)

(圣人用《周易》卦爻来察见天下万物的奥妙，从而模拟万物的形态，象征事物之所宜，所以称之为象。)

Sages use the hexagrams and trigrams described in *The Book of Changes* to observe the subtleties of all things under heaven and determine what is fitting through the simulation of shapes in different things. Therefore it is called *xiang* (images). (*The Book of Changes*)

xiǎoshuō 小说

Fiction

以人物形象刻画为中心，通过完整的故事情节和环境描写来反映社会生活的一种文学体式。人物、情节、环境是小说的三要素。按照篇幅及容量，小说可分为长篇、中篇、短篇。中国古典小说，按照所表现的内容，可分为神怪小说、历史演义小说、英雄传奇小说、世情小说等几大类；按照体制可分为笔记体、传奇体、话本体、章回体等；按照语言形式，可分为文言小说和白话小说。中国古典小说经过了不同的发展阶段，有着鲜明的时代特点：先秦两汉时期的神话传说、史传文学，以及诸子散文中的寓言故事等，是中国古代小说的源头；魏晋南北朝时期出现的文人笔记小说，是中国古代小说的雏形；唐代传奇标志着古典小说的正式形成；宋、元出现的话本小说，为小说的成熟奠定了坚实的基础；明清小说标志着中国古典小说发展的高峰，出现了《三国演义》《水浒传》《西游记》《红楼梦》等古典名著。"五四"新文化运动之后，现代白话小说创作大量涌现，传播着现代的科学与民主精神。

Fiction is a literary genre primarily concerned with depicting characters to tell a complete story about social life within a setting. Fiction has three main elements, namely, characters, a plot, and a setting. Depending on the length, fiction can be divided into novels, novellas, and short stories. In terms of content, traditional Chinese fiction can be divided into the following broad categories: fantasy stories of gods and spirits, historical fiction, heroic legendary tales, and stories about human relations and social mores. In terms of genre, traditional Chinese fiction is divided into literary sketches, legendary tales, story-tellers' prompt-books, and chapter-based novels. In terms of language, there is fiction in the classical language and vernacular fiction. Traditional Chinese fiction has evolved through different stages, with distinctive features for each period. The myths, legends and historical biographies of the pre-Qin and Han dynasties, and the fables in the works of the earlier Chinese thinkers were the sources of traditional Chinese fiction. The literary sketches by men of letters in the Wei, Jin, Northern and Southern dynasties were embryonic forms of traditional fiction. The legendary tales of the Tang Dynasty marked the eventual emergence of Chinese fiction. The story-tellers' prompt-books in the Song and Yuan dynasties laid the foundation that allowed traditional fiction to reach maturity. The novels of the Ming and Qing dynasties marked the peak in the development of pre-modern fiction. That period is famous for producing great Chinese classical novels, namely, *Romance of the Three Kingdoms*, *Journey to the West*, *Outlaws of the Marsh* and *Dream of the Red Chamber*. During and after the New Culture Movement and the May 4th Movement around 1919, a large amount of modern vernacular fiction appeared, bringing forth a message of science and democracy of the modern age.

引例 Citations：

◎若其小说家合丛残小语，近取譬论，以作短书，治身理家，有可观之辞。(《昭明文选》卷三十一李善注引桓谭《新论》)
(像那些小说家将零散的论述整合起来，用身边发生的事情打比方进行述说劝诫，所写文章都不长，其中论述个人修身和治理家庭的内容，有不少可看的地方。)

Those writers of stories put together scattered statements. Drawing on what happens around them, they make up parables, writing short pieces. The parts about how to improve one's character and keep good family life are worth reading. (Huan Tan: *New Treatise,* as cited in *Selections of Refined Literature Compiled by Prince Zhaoming*, Vol. 31 Li Shan's Note)

◎小说，正史之余也。(笑花主人《〈今古奇观〉序》)
(小说，是正史之外的一种文学形式。)

Fiction is a literary supplement to formal historical accounts. (Xiaohua Zhuren: Foreword to *Strange Tales New and Old*)

xiěyì 写意

Freehand Brushwork

中国画表现手法之一。以简练恣纵的笔墨勾勒描绘物象的意态神韵，重在抒发创作主体的意兴情趣。用笔灵活，不拘工细，不求形似（与"工笔"相对）。写意看似草率随意，实则谨严而内蕴法度，不仅要求画家在创作前对物象进行深入的观察和体验，营构好画面中诸多物象的位置关系，而且还须具备精深娴熟的技法功底，才能意居笔先而神出形外。写意有小写意、大写意之分，后者多采用泼墨技法。写意对后来的戏曲创作及表演手法有较大影响。戏曲中的写意，主要通过虚拟性、程式化的动作，并融合一定的歌舞表演来呈现舞台艺术的审美意象。

Freehand brushwork is one of the traditional methods of brushwork expression in Chinese painting. Using abbreviated and willful brushwork, the artist suggests graphically the meaning and character of the object and its shape. The chief aim is to give rein to the artist's subjective state and mood. It stresses flexibility in brushwork, unrestrained by unimportant details and rejecting naturalistic effects (in contrast with meticulous painting). This style of painting, while seemingly coarse and whimsical, is in fact highly conscious of, and strictly consistent with, standards of artistic creation. Besides demanding close observation and experience of natural objects prior to painting, such as that the various forms within the picture will be laid out appropriately, it also demands solid technical proficiency in order that the artistic intent be formed in imagination before taking shape in painting. Freehand brushwork is divided into greater freehand and lesser freehand, with the former often employing the ink-splashing technique. It had a significant influence on the production of operas and the development of acting techniques in later ages. The freehand style in Chinese-style opera is shown through consciously artificial, stylized motions, accompanied by singing and dancing, to present images artistically on the stage.

引例 Citations：

◎僧仲仁……以墨晕作梅，如花影然，别成一家，所谓写意者也。（夏文彦

《图绘宝鉴》卷三）

（僧人仲仁……通过渲染墨晕来画梅花，仿佛花影一般，这种画法自成一家，称得上是写意高手。）

By applying washes without lines, the Buddhist monk Zhongren painted plum blossoms which looked like florid shadows, thus creating a distinctive style of his own. This is what is meant by freehand brushwork! (Xia Wenyan: *The Precious Mirror of Painting*)

◎ 世以画蔬果、花草随手点簇者，谓之写意；细笔钩染者，谓之写生。（方薰《山静居画论》卷下）

（世人将随手点染而画出蔬菜、瓜果、花草的称作"写意"，将用细致工整的笔法钩描实物的称作"写生"。）

People describe paintings of vegetables, fruits, plants, and flowers painted according to the artist's whim, with dots here and there, "freehand brushwork," whereas they see paintings in the detailed style as "naturalistic drawings." (Fang Xun: *On Painting in the Quiet Mountain Studio*)

xīnzhī 心知

Mind Cognition

基于心的一种认识活动。由于人们对心及其与外物关系的理解不同，因此对"心知"的认识也有所差异。有人强调，人需要通过心的作用认识日用伦常之道，并使之成为某种内在的诉求。"心知"是人实现道德行为与伦理生活的必要条件。而人心时常处于被遮蔽或不确定的状态，只有通过对心的培养与引导，才能发挥其应有的作用。但也有人认为，"心知"会使人焦灼于变动、繁复的外物，从而造成生命的不安。因此需要排除"心知"，使心进入虚静的状态，不受外物的干扰。

The term means cognitive activities of the mind. As there are different views on the relationship between the mind and the external world, people's understanding of the mind's cognitive process also varies. Some people emphasize the role of the mind in shaping ethical standards in daily life and making them a source of inner strength. Cognition of the mind is a prerequisite for moral cultivation and ethical living. As the mind is often in a blocked or unstable state, it needs to be nurtured with proper guidance before it can play its due role. However, others argue that the mind's cognitive activities make one concerned about the evolving complexity of the external world and feel anxious about life. It is therefore necessary to get rid of the mind's cognitive activities so as to leave the mind in a state of tranquility free from outside interference.

引例 Citation：

◎人何以知道？曰：心。心何以知？曰：虚壹而静。(《荀子·解蔽》)
(人如何能够知晓道？回答：用心。心如何能够知晓？回答：做到"虚壹而静"。)

How can people learn to know Dao? The answer is to use one's heart and mind. How can the heart and mind know? The answer is to achieve open-mindedness, concentration, and tranquility. (*Xunzi*)

xíngxiān-zhīhòu 行先知后

First Action, Then Knowledge

对"知""行"关系的一种认识。王夫之(1619—1692)等人在"知""行"关系问题上提出了"行先知后"的主张。王夫之承认对人伦日用之道的体认与践行是相互关联的,但就先后而言,只有先"行"才能获得"知"。"行"是"知"的来源,对"知"起着决定性的作用。能"行"必然对所行之事有所"知",但能"知"却未必能"行"。

The term represents one interpretation of the relationship between "knowledge" and "action." Regarding the relationship between "knowledge" and "action," Wang Fuzhi (1619-1692) and others argued that "action precedes knowledge." Wang acknowledged that an understanding of the principles underlying human relations in everyday life is interrelated with the application of these principles, but in terms of sequence, only through "action" can one obtain "knowledge." "Action" is the source of "knowledge" and has a decisive impact on "knowledge." If one can "act," one inevitably "knows" about one's actions, but the ability to "know" does not necessarily translate into the ability to "act."

引例 Citation：

◎行焉而后知其艰,非力行焉者不能知也。(王夫之《四书训义·论语九》)
(践行之后才知道其中的艰难,若没有努力践行就不能知晓。)

Only after acting can one know the difficulties involved; without efforts to act one cannot know. (Wang Fuzhi: *Explicating the Lessons of the Four Books*) xuán 玄

***Xuan* (Mystery)**

原义为幽深玄妙，用以描述万物的本原状态。老子用它形容"道""德"的幽深玄妙，称"道""玄之又玄"，又倡"玄德"。扬雄（前53—公元18）、葛洪（281？—341）等人则进一步将"玄"描述为天地万物的最高本原或本体。在这个意义上，"玄"是超越一切具体事物、无形无象的某种绝对存在。后世有"玄学"之称，指探讨世界本原或本体的学问。

The term first described the original state of everything, which is profound and mysterious. Laozi used it to describe Dao and virtue as being in a profound and mysterious state, calling Dao "a mystery within a mystery," and advocating "inconspicuous virtue." Ancient Chinese thinkers like Yang Xiong (53 BC-AD 18) and Ge Hong (281?-341) went a step further, describing *xuan* (玄) as being the supreme original source or the primal ontological existence of all things in heaven and on earth. In this sense *xuan* is a kind of absolute existence, formless and imageless, which transcends all concrete things. Later on, *xuanxue* (玄学), or learning of the mystery, developed, referring to the quest into the original source or ontological existence of the world.

引例 Citations：

◎此两者同出而异名，同谓之玄，玄之又玄，众妙之门。(《老子·一章》)
（有与无有共同的出处而名称不同，都是深奥玄妙的，极为深奥玄妙，是一切变化的门径。）

You and *wu* are from the same origin but have different names. They are all extremely mysterious and profound and lead to all changes. (*Laozi*)

◎玄者，自然之始祖，而万殊之大宗也。（葛洪《抱朴子·畅玄》）

（"玄"是自然的端始，是各种不同事物的本原。）

Xuan is the origin of nature and the source of all things. (Ge Hong: *Baopuzi*)

xuèqì 血气

Vitality / Vital Force

反映着人与动物的身体需求与生命状态的气。"血气"是人天生所具有的，反映着血肉之躯对于外在物质的需求。"血气"的状态在人的各个生命阶段中是不同的，其盛衰反映着生命力的强弱。年轻时"血气"并不稳定，及至壮年则"血气"强盛，年老则"血气"衰弱。此外，不同人的"血气"强弱程度也有所差异。有的人"血气"刚强，有的则较为柔和。"血气"可以通过礼乐教化而加以改变。同时，"血气"也构成人的道德情感发生的基础。

The term refers to vitality which is needed for the human or animal body to sustain its life and which reflects the state of life. It is something one is born with, representing the body's needs of material things. A person exhibits different levels of vitality at different stages of life, reflecting changes in the strength of life. Vitality is unstable in youth; it reaches its peak in the prime of life, and in old age it wanes. Furthermore, different people have different levels of vitality, some overflowing with vigor, while others are subdued. People's vitality can be changed by means of rites, music and through education; it is the basis for shaping a person's moral and emotional trait.

引例 Citations：

◎ 孔子曰："君子有三戒：少之时，血气未定，戒之在色；及其壮也，血气方刚，戒之在斗；及其老也，血气既衰，戒之在得。"（《论语·季氏》）

（孔子说："君子有三件事应该警惕戒备：年轻的时候，血气不稳定，要戒备迷恋美色；等到壮年，血气旺盛，要戒备好勇斗狠；到了老年，血气已经衰弱，要戒备贪得无厌。"）

Confucius said, "One should guard against three things in life. In his youth his vital force is unstable and he should guard against lust. As his vital force strengthens in the prime of life, he should guard against aggressive behavior. In his old age his vital force weakens, and he should guard against greed." (*The Analects*)

◎ 凡生乎天地之间者，有血气之属必有知，有知之属莫不爱其类。（《荀子·礼论》）

（凡是生于天地之间的人和物，只要有血气的就必然会有知觉，有知觉的没有不亲爱其同类的。）

All things born between heaven and earth with vital force have consciousness; and with consciousness they all love their own kind. (*Xunzi*)

xúnmíng-zéshí 循名责实

Hold Actualities According to Its Name

依据名而衡量其所指之实。"循名责实"是古人治理国家的重要手段。在现实的人伦关系中，每一个特定的角色或身份都有其名，名也即规定了这一角色或身份应该具有的性质或职责。对使用或拥有某一名分的人，需要依据其名分考核、要求其实际的言行与名所规定的性质或职责相符。

An actual object should be assessed according to the name referring to it. Holding actualities according to its name was an important means for ancient Chinese to govern the state. In actual human relations concerning ethics and morality, every specific role or status had its name, which determined the character or responsibilities of that status. People with certain status had to be assessed on the basis of their status, and it was required that their actual words and actions corresponded to the character and responsibilities determined by the name of their status.

引例 Citations：

◎术者，因任而授官，循名而责实，操杀生之柄，课群臣之能者也。(《韩非子·定法》)
（所谓术，是根据个人的能力而授予官职，依照官职名分而要求其履行相应的职责，掌握生杀大权，考量群臣中能力出众的人。）

The way of governance is to bestow office according to responsibilities, who was required to carry out duties as was required by the name (i.e. the office), to exercise power over life and death, and examine and weigh officials with outstanding capabilities. (*Hanfeizi*)

◎循名责实，实之极也；按实定名，名之极也。(《邓析子·转辞》)
（依据名而衡量其所指之实，是要求实的标准；依据实在的内容去确定事物的名号，是要求名的标准。）

To assess the actual thing or substance according to its name means to demand an actual standard. To determine the name of a thing or substance according to actualities is the standard for naming the name. (*Dengxizi*)

yǎyuè 雅乐

Fine Music

典雅纯正的音乐。是古代帝王祭祀天地、祖先，举行朝贺、宫廷宴享及其他重大庆典活动时所用的音乐。"雅乐"多歌颂朝廷功德，音乐中正平和，歌词典雅纯正，其奏唱、伴舞都有明确的礼仪规范。历代朝廷都将雅乐作为推行教化、感化民风的重要手段。雅乐作为宫廷音乐，有保守的一面，但在实际历史发展中也注意吸收民间歌舞、异域歌舞的成分而不断创新，因而代表着不同时代的音乐最高水准。唐以后雅乐传入日本、韩国、越南等国，成为这些国家的乐舞文化的重要组成部分。

The term refers to a kind of classical music in China. Noble and pure, it was the music used by kings in ancient times when worshipping heaven, earth, and ancestors, receiving congratulations from other quarters of the world, or holding feasts and major ceremonial activities. Chinese classical music often eulogized the royal court's accomplishments; its melodies were tranquil and stately, its wording elegant and tasteful, and its performance of song and dance followed explicit codes of etiquette. Rulers of all dynasties used this kind of music as an effective means to instruct their people and promote civic virtue. As a courtly tradition, the music was necessarily conservative. However, throughout history the assimilation of elements of folk song and dance, as well as the music and dance of foreign lands, inevitably led to innovation. Thus, it maintained throughout the ages the highest levels of musical excellence. After the Tang Dynasty, this kind of music spread to other Asian countries such as Japan, Korea, and Vietnam, becoming a constituent part of their musical culture.

引例 Citations：

◎子曰："恶紫之夺朱也，恶郑声之乱雅乐也，恶利口之覆邦家者也。"(《论语·阳货》)

(孔子说："我厌恶用紫色取代红色，厌恶用郑国的音乐扰乱雅正的音乐，憎恶伶牙俐齿而使国家倾覆的人。")

Confucius said, "I detest replacing red with purple and interfering refined classical music with the music of the State of Zheng. I loathe those who overthrow the state with their glib tongues." (*The Analects*)

◎是时，河间献王有雅材，亦以为治道非礼乐不成，因献所集雅乐。(《汉书·礼乐志》)

(当时，河间献王有很高的才能，他也认为治国之道如果没有礼乐就不完备，于是就把他所收集的雅乐献给了朝廷。)

At the time, Liu De, Prince Xian of Hejian, was an exceptionally talented man, and he believed that music and ceremony were essential to the proper governing of the state. As a result he donated all the documents of classical music he had collected to the court. (*The History of the Han Dynasty*)

◎荀勖(xù)善解音声，时论谓之闇(ān)解。遂调律吕，正雅乐。(刘义庆《世说新语·术解》)

(荀勖善于辨音，时人认为他有音乐天赋。于是朝廷让他负责调整音律、校定雅乐。)

Xun Xu had a sensitive ear for musical tones. Some, recognizing his musical gift, recommended him for a position overseeing musical rules and revising classical music. (Liu Yiqing: *A New Account of Tales of the World*)

yánbùjìnyì 言不尽意

Words Cannot Fully Express Thought.

言语不能完全表达对世界的根本认识。语出《周易·系辞上》,指语言在表意上有所不足,因而设立卦象来表达圣人之意。荀粲(209?—238)、王弼(226—249)等魏晋玄学家进一步阐发了这一思想。他们对语言与思想关系的认识,是由其对世界本体或本原的理解所决定的。他们认为,世界的本体或本原是超越于有形事物之上的"无"。"无"没有具体的形态或属性,也就无法被命名和言说。因此,言语对思想的表达被认为是有局限的。

Words cannot fully express the fundamental understanding of the world. According to *The Book of Changes*, words are inadequate for expressing what one means and that was why the hexagram images were made to convey the ideas of the sages. Xun Can (209?-238), Wang Bi (226-249), and other metaphysicians of the Wei and Jin dynasties further elucidated this concept. Their understanding of the relationship between language and thinking was determined by their understanding of the ontological existence or original source of the world. They believed that the world's ontological existence or original source was *wu* (无), which was beyond anything tangible. *Wu* had no specific form or attribute, and it was therefore impossible to name or describe it. Thus, language was found to have its limitations in expressing thought.

引例 Citations:

◎书不尽言,言不尽意。(《周易·系辞上》)

(书面文字不能完全表达作者的语言及全部意义,语言也不能完全表达作者心中所想及全部认识。）

Written characters cannot fully express what the author wants to say, nor can words fully express his thought and knowledge. (*The Book of Changes*)

◎斯则象外之意，《系》表之言，固蕴而不出矣。(《三国志·魏书·荀彧传附子恽》裴松之注引）

（[这是]卦象之外的思想、《系辞》之外的言辞，本来就是蕴藏其中而无法用言辞文字能够表达的。）

The notions beyond the images and the words beyond "The Great Treatise" are deeply stored in them, and so they cannot be expressed. (As Cited in Pei Songzhi: *Annotations on The History of the Three Kingdoms*)

yánjìnyì 言尽意

Words Can Fully Express Thought.

　　言语能够表达对世界的根本认识。言语与思想的关系是魏晋时人讨论的一个重要议题。欧阳建（？—300）不满于荀粲（209？—238）、王弼（226—249）等人的"言不尽意"的看法，提出了"言尽意"的主张。在他看来，"意"（思想）是对事物及其道理的认识。而名号、言语则是对"物"（事物）、"理"（事理）的反映，由"物""理"而定。"意"的获得与表达是通过名号、言语的辨析而实现的。"意"与"言"是一致的，不能割裂。因此，"意"可以全面、透彻地表达思想认识。

Words can fully express the fundamental understanding of the universe. The relationship between language and thought was a prominent topic of debate in the Wei and Jin dynasties. Ouyang Jian (?-300) did not accept the view of Xun Can (209?-238) and Wang Bi (226-249), who alleged that "words cannot fully express thought." Instead, he put forward the notion that "words can fully express thought." In his opinion, thought represents perceptions of objects and reason, while names and words are reflections of them and are determined by things and reason. As a thought is acquired and expressed, it is analyzed and realized by names and words. Thoughts and their correspondent words are in accord with each other and inseparable. Thus thought can be fully and exhaustively expressed.

引例 Citation：

◎名逐物而迁，言因理而变，此犹声发响应，形存影附，不得相与为二，苟其不二，则无不尽，吾故以为尽矣。(《艺文类聚》卷十九"言语"引欧阳建《尽意论》)

（名号依循事物而变化，言语依据事理而改变，这就如同声音发出就有回声响应，形体存在就有影子附着，不能析为两个东西，如果二者不分离，则名号、言语没有不能表达的事物和事理，我因此认为言语完全能够表达自己的思想。）

Names change when the objects they refer to change. Language changes on the basis of reason. That is like the echo responding to a sound or a shadow following a shape. They are not to be considered as separate things. If they are not separate things, then there is nothing that cannot be fully expressed. Therefore, I believe language can fully express thought. (Ouyang Jian: On Fully Expressing Ideas)

Yán-Huáng 炎黄

The Fiery Emperor and the Yellow Emperor / Emperor Yan and Emperor Huang

炎帝和黄帝。是历史传说中上古的两个帝王，亦即两个部落首领。炎帝姓姜，号"神农氏"；黄帝姓公孙，号"轩辕氏"。他们居住在中原，与东方部落和南方部落逐渐融合，不断繁衍，形成华夏族主体（汉朝以后称为汉族，唐朝以后又称唐人），因而他们被尊为华夏民族的祖先。他们的部落尤其是黄帝部落，文明程度最高，上古的许多重要的文化、技术发明都是由他们两个部落创造的，因而他们又被视为华夏文明的始祖。近代以后，他们又成为整个中华民族和中华文明的一种象征。至今散居世界各地的华裔也大多认同自己是"炎黄子孙"或"黄帝子孙"。"炎黄"实际上已成为中华民族共同的文化符号。

Emperor Yan (the Fiery Emperor) and Emperor Huang (the Yellow Emperor), legendary Chinese rulers in pre-dynastic times, were actually tribal leaders. Emperor Yan, whose family name was Jiang, was known as Shennongshi while Emperor Huang, whose family name was Gongsun, was known as Xuanyuanshi. They originally lived in central China where their tribes gradually merged with those in eastern and southern China. People in these tribes proliferated and made up the main body of the Chinese nation (who were referred to as the Han people after the Han Dynasty and Tang people after the Tang Dynasty). Hence, they have been revered as the ancestors of the Chinese nation. Their tribes, and the tribe headed by the Yellow Emperor in particular, achieved the highest level of civilization. Many important cultural advancements and technical innovations in ancient China were believed to be created by these two tribes. They have therefore been seen as the forefathers of the Chinese civilization. In modern times, they have been considered as symbols of the Chinese nation and Chinese culture. Today, Chinese descendants residing in different parts of the world proudly regard themselves as "descendants of the Fiery Emperor and the Yellow Emperor" or simply "descendants of the Yellow Emperor." In this regard, "Yan and Huang" have become cultural symbols of the Chinese nation.

引例 Citations：

◎周室既坏，至春秋末，诸侯秏尽，而炎黄唐虞之苗裔尚犹颇有存者。(《汉书·魏豹、田儋（dān）、韩王信传赞》)

（周天子的统治秩序已经崩溃，至春秋末期，诸侯国消灭殆尽，但炎黄尧舜的后代仍大有人在。）

With the collapse of the ruling order of the emperors of the Zhou Dynasty, by the end of the Spring and Autumn Period, various vassal states had been defeated, but numerous descendants of Emperors Yan, Huang, Yao, and Shun remained. (*The History of the Han Dynasty*)

◎我们大家都是许身革命的黄帝子孙。(国民政府《告抗战全体将士书》)

We, descendants of the Fiery Emperor and the Yellow Emperor, have devoted ourselves to the revolution. ("To All Officers and Soldiers Fighting the War Against Japanese Aggression" issued by the then national government of China)

yīwù-liǎngtǐ 一物两体

One Thing in Two Fundamental States

作为统一体的"气"之中包含着对立的两个方面。张载（1020—1077）认为，天地万物都是由"气"构成的。"气"是完整的统一体，也即"一物"。同时，"气"又有虚实、动静、聚散、清浊等对立的状态，即是"两体"。没有对立面的相互作用，则没有统一体的存在；没有统一体的存在，则对立的相互作用也会消失。统一体之中的对立，是"气"及其所构成的事物产生变化的根源。

Qi (气), or vital force, consists of two opposing aspects. According to the Song-dynasty philosopher Zhang Zai (1020-1077), everything in the world consists of *qi*. On the one hand, *qi* is a whole and one thing; on the other, it consists of pairs of contradictory states, such as the real and the unreal, motion and stillness, concentration and diffusion, and clarity and opacity. Without interaction between the opposite states, the whole cannot exist. Likewise, without the whole, there can be no interaction between the opposite states. Contradictions within the whole constitute the source of changes of *qi* and all things made of *qi*.

引例 Citation：

◎一物两体，气也。一故神，两故化，此天之所以参（sān）也。（张载《正蒙·参两》）

（统一的事物之中包含着对立的两个方面，这就是"气"的状态。作为统一体，因此有神妙的运动。两个对立面相互作用，因此有无穷的变化。这也就是天所具有的"三"的意义。）

One thing with two states, that is *qi*, or vital force. As one whole thing, *qi* has miraculous movements, caused by interaction between the two opposites; and such movements create endless changes. This is why heaven has three aspects (the whole and the two states). (Zhang Zai: *Enlightenment Through Confucian Teachings*)

yǐ wú wéi běn 以无为本

Wu Is the Origin.

将"无"作为世界的本体或本原。老子曾提出"有生于无"。魏晋时期的何晏（？—249）、王弼（226—249）等人进一步发挥这一思想，主张天地万物都"以无为本"。他们认为，任何具体的事物都不能作为另外一个具体事物的本体或本原，更不能成为整个世界的本体或本原。天地万物的发生与存在都依赖于一个更根本的、超越于有形事物之上的"无"。只有无形无名的本体才能使众多的具体事物发挥各自的功用。

Wu (无) is regarded as the original source or ontological existence of the world in classical Chinese thinking. Laozi claimed that "*you* (有) is born out of *wu*." This concept was further developed by He Yan (?-249), Wang Bi (226-249), and other thinkers of the Wei and Jin dynasties, who maintained that heaven, earth, and all things in the world originate from *wu*. No specific being, they argued, can be the original source or ontological existence of another being, much less of the world. The formation and existence of everything depend on *wu*, which is the fundamental source that transcends all tangible beings. Only an intangible and unidentifiable ontological existence gives countless specific beings their functions.

引例 Citation：

◎天下之物，皆以有为生。有之所始，以无为本。将欲全有，必反于无也。（王弼《老子注》）

（天下的事物都以有形的状态存在着，有形之物的发生，以"无"作为其本体。想要保全有形之物，必须返归于"无"。）

All things under heaven exist by means of *you*. The formation and existence of *you* originate from *wu*. To maintain *you* we must return to *wu*. (Wang Bi: *Annotations on Laozi*)

yǐzhí-bàoyuàn 以直报怨

Repay a Grudge with Rectitude

　　以正直之道对待怨恨的人。"以直报怨"是孔子（前551—前479）提出的一种报答仇怨的原则。对待怨恨的人，孔子认为"以怨报怨""以德报怨"这两种处理方式都不正确。孔子主张，不可因一时的愤恨情绪而肆意施加报复，也不可隐匿仇怨报答以恩惠友善，而应该分辨造成仇怨之事的是非曲直，以正直的原则做出回应。

Treat a person you hold a grudge against with upright behavior. "Repaying a grudge with rectitude" was a principle proposed by Confucius (551-479 BC) for dealing with grudges. He felt that both "repaying a grudge with a grudge" and "repaying a grudge with kindness" were incorrect. Confucius argued that one should not deliberately seek vengeance out of momentary anger, nor should one conceal resentment over a grudge and repay it with kindness. Rather, one should analyze the rights and wrongs of the episode which created the grudge, and respond according to the principles of rectitude.

引例 Citation：

◎ 或曰："以德报怨，何如？"子曰："何以报德？以直报怨，以德报德。"(《论语·宪问》)

(有人说："以恩惠友善来报答怨恨之人，怎么样呢？"孔子说："用什么来报答有恩德之人呢？应以正直之道回应怨恨之人，以恩惠友善回应有恩德之人。")

Someone asked, "How about repaying a grudge with kindness?" Confucius said, "Then how would you repay kindness? Repay a grudge with rectitude, and repay kindness with kindness." (*The Analects*)

yǒuróng-nǎidà 有容乃大

A Broad Mind Achieves Greatness.

有包容，才能有大成就。"有容"即器量大，能包容一切；"大"指气魄、事业伟大。"有容"是一种道德修养，更是一种生存智慧。它是在承认并尊重个体及社会差异基础上调处自我与他人关系、寻求社会和谐的一种道德自觉，但又不是故意纵容或作无原则的妥协。"有容乃大"提醒人们立身行事尤其是为官理政，要心胸开阔，善于听取各种意见，宽和对待不同事物，就像大海接纳无数江河细流一样，这样才能养成伟大的品格，成就伟大的事业。其义与"厚德载物"相通。

A broad mind achieves greatness. *Yourong* (有容) means that one has the capacity to accommodate others. *Da* (大) refers to great courage and an important cause. *Yourong* is a moral standard, and more importantly, contains wisdom for survival. It is a conscious act of morality in pursuit of social harmony by managing and regulating relations between oneself and others on the basis of recognizing and respecting individual and social differences, without resorting to deliberate connivance or making unprincipled compromise. The term teaches people how to conduct themselves, particularly officials in exercising their administrative powers. That is, they should have a broad mind, open to different views and different things, like the sea accepting numerous rivers flowing into it. This is the way to cultivate great character and important achievements. Its meaning is similar to the term *houde-zaiwu* (厚德载物 have ample virtue and carry all things).

引例 **Citations**：

◎必有忍，其乃有济。有容，德乃大。(《尚书·君陈》)
(必须有所忍耐，才能有所成就。有包容，才能建立大功德。)

Tolerance and patience lead people to success, and broad-mindedness to merits and virtues. (*The Book of History*)

◎海纳百川，有容乃大；壁立千仞，无欲则刚。(林则徐对联)
(大海广阔接纳无数江河，人有度量才能 [像大海那样] 有大成就；千仞崖壁巍然屹立，人没有贪欲就能 [像山崖那样] 刚正凛然。)

The vast ocean accepts hundreds of rivers emptying into it; people with a broad mind can achieve greatness. Thousands of cliffs stand tall and lofty; people with no covetous desires stand firm and upright. (A couplet composed by Lin Zexu)

yǔmín-gēngshǐ 与民更始

Make a Fresh Start with the People

和民众一起革新政治。更始：重新开始。原指帝王即位改元或采取某些重大措施，后指执政者与民众一起变革现状，开创新局面。其中蕴含着悠远深厚的民本思想和君民一体、上下一心、共同革故鼎新的精神。

The term means to make political reform together with the people. *Gengshi* (更始) means to make a fresh start. The term used to refer to a new emperor ascending the throne, taking a new reign title or implementing a series of new policies. Later, it came to mean that the rulers worked together with the people trying to change the status quo and opening up new prospects. The term reflects a profound and far-reaching thought of putting people first, and highlights the spirit of monarchs and the people working with one heart and one mind to abolish what is old and establish in its place a new order.

引例 Citation：

◎朕嘉唐虞而乐殷周，据旧以鉴新，其赦天下，与民更始。(《汉书·武帝纪》)

（我赞美尧、舜而喜欢商、周，依据旧时做法并参照新规，下诏给所有罪犯免刑或减刑，和百姓一起开创新局面。）

I praise ancient emperors Yao and Shun; I like the Shang and Zhou dynasties. I have issued an imperial decree to either exempt criminals from punishment or commute their sentences on the basis of the old practice and new rules, so that we may open up a new era together with the people. (*The History of the Han Dynasty*)

zàizhōu-fùzhōu 载舟覆舟

Carry or Overturn the Boat / Make or Break

　　水既能载船航行，也能使船倾覆。"水"比喻百姓，"舟"比喻统治者。"载舟覆舟"所昭示的是民心向背的重要性：人民才是决定政权存亡、国家兴衰的根本力量。这与"民惟邦本""顺天应人"的政治思想是相通的。自古以来它对执政者有积极的警示作用，提醒他们尊重民情民意，执政为民，居安思危。

Water can carry a boat, but can also overturn it. Here, water is compared to the people, while the boat is compared to the ruler. The phrase, "carry or overturn the boat," reveals the importance of popular support: people are the critical force that decides the future of a regime and a country. This is consistent with such political doctrines as "people are the foundation of the state," and "follow the mandate of heaven and comply with the wishes of the people." Since ancient times, this term has served as a warning to the ruler, reminding him of the need to respect local conditions and popular will, to govern the country for the people, and to anticipate dangers in times of security.

引例 Citation：

◎君者，舟也；庶人者，水也。水则载舟，水则覆舟，此之谓也。(《荀子·王制》)

（君主是船，百姓是水。水既能载船航行，也能使船倾覆，说的就是这个道理。）

The ruler is the boat and the people are the water. Water can carry the boat but can also overturn it. This is the very truth. (*Xunzi*)

zhèngmíng 正名

Rectification of Names

修正或端正事物的指称、名号，使名实相符。"名"是对事物的指称，规定着事物的属性及其与他者的关系。"实"是名所指称的事物、实体。名的规定应与其所指之实相符。但在现实中，名实往往不能相合。针对这种情况，就要求事物所用之名不能超过事物自身的属性，名所指之实也不能超出名所规定的范围。"正名"是维护名所构建的社会秩序的重要方法。各家都认同"正名"的主张，但其所修正的"名"的具体内容则有所不同。

This refers to the rectification of what things are called so that name and reality correspond. A name is what is used to refer to a thing, which determines the attributes of the thing and its relations with other things. "Reality" refers to a thing or an entity that its name refers to. The name of a thing should conform to what the thing actually is. However, very often name and reality do not match in real life. To deal with this situation, the name of a thing should not go beyond the nature of the thing; likewise, the reality referred to by the name must not go beyond the scope that the name implies. The "rectification of names" is an important way to maintain the social order constructed by the names. Various schools of thoughts have agreed on the necessity of rectifying names, but they differ in their views of the concrete meanings of the names to be rectified.

引例 Citations：

◎名不正，则言不顺；言不顺，则事不成；事不成，则礼乐不兴；礼乐不兴，则刑罚不中；刑罚不中，则民无所错手足。(《论语·子路》)

（名号不端正，则说话就不能顺畅；说话不顺畅，则做事就不能成功；做事不成功，则礼乐就不能兴盛；礼乐不兴盛，则刑罚就不能得当；刑罚不得当，则百姓就不知所措。）

If names are not rectified, one's argument will not be proper. If speech is not proper, nothing can be accomplished. If nothing is accomplished, rites and music will not flourish. If rites and music do not flourish, punishments will not be meted out properly. If punishments are not meted out properly, people will have no guidance as how to behave. (*The Analects*)

◎其正者，正其所实也；正其所实者，正其名也。(《公孙龙子·名实论》)
（所要正的，就是端正名所指称的实；端正名所指称的实，就是正名。）

Rectification is to bring forth what actuality is. To bring forth what actuality is is what it means to rectify the name. (*Gongsunlongzi*)

zhèngxīn 正心

Rectify One's Heart / Mind

使心归之于正以践行日用伦常之道。出自《礼记·大学》，与格物、致知、诚意、修身、齐家、治国、平天下并称"八条目"，是儒家所倡导的道德修养的一个重要环节。"正心"以"诚意"为前提。在真诚践行日用伦常之道的过程中，人心不可避免地会因愤怒、恐惧、欢乐、忧患等情感而有所偏邪。因此需要时常修正自己的心意，使之不受干扰，始终保持对实现日用伦常之道的追求。

This term means to rectify our mind so as to follow moral principles in daily life. Rectifying one's heart or mind is one of the eight notions from the philosophical text *The Great Learning* (a section of *The Book of Rites*), the other seven being "studying things," "acquiring knowledge," "being sincere in thought," "cultivating oneself," "regulating one's family well," "governing the state properly," and "bringing peace to all under heaven." These constitute important stages in the moral cultivation advocated by the Confucian school. "Rectifying one's mind" has as its preceding stage "being sincere in thought." In the course of following the moral principles earnestly in daily life, people are inevitably influenced by sentiments such as anger, fear, joy, and worries, which will, to some degree, lead a person astray. Therefore, one must always try to rectify one's mind and avoid being swayed by any interference, so as to keep to the observance of moral principles in daily life.

引例 Citations：

◎意既诚了，而其心或有所偏倚，则不得其正，故方可做那正心底工夫。(《朱子语类》卷十六)
("诚意"已经做到了，而心意或许有所偏颇，就不能做到端正，因此正可做"正心"方面的锻炼。)

When thought has been made sincere but the mind is perhaps still somewhat biased, then it is not possible for a person to stay pure and unbiased. Therefore one should make efforts to rectify one's mind. (*Categorized Conversations of Master Zhu Xi*)

◎著（zhuó）实致其良知而无一毫意、必、固、我，便是正心。(《传习录》卷中)
(切实地发挥良知而没有一丝妄测、武断、固执、自我之心，这便是"正心"。)

To rectify one's mind means to cultivate one's good conscience without the least conjecture, arbitrariness, stubbornness, or egoism. (*Records of Great Learning*)

zhèngzhě-zhèngyě 政者正也

Governance Means Rectitude.

"政"就是"正"的意思。"政"即政治、治理国家;"正"即坚持原则,端正品行,处事公正。"政者正也"有两层意思:一是强调为政者在施政层面应坚持原则、端正品行、处事公正;二是在道德层面强调为政者应严格要求自己,通过自身的示范作用,影响下属和民众一起循行正道、遵守社会规范。它是古代"人治""德政"思想的具体体现。

Zheng (政), or governance, refers to policy and managing the country, while *zheng* (正), or rectitude, refers to adherence to principle, decent behavior, and handling matters with fairness. This term has two meanings. First, it emphasizes that those who govern should adhere to principle, behave correctly, and handle matters with fairness. Second, it emphasizes that at a moral level, those who govern should be strict with themselves, that they should play an exemplary role and thus show their subordinates and the people how to follow the right path and comply with social norms. It is a concrete expression of the idea "rule by man" and "governing by virtue" in ancient times.

引例 Citations:

◎季康子问政于孔子,孔子对曰:"政者,正也。子帅以正,孰敢不正?"(《论语·颜渊》)

(季康子问孔子如何治理国家。孔子回答说:"政就是正的意思。您本人带头走正道，谁敢不跟着走正道呢？"）

When asked by Ji Kang about governance, Confucius replied, "Governance is all about rectitude. If you lead along the right path, who would dare not to follow you?" (*The Analects*)

◎子曰："其身正，不令而行；其不正，虽令不从。"（《论语·子路》）
（孔子说："执政者自身行为端正，即使不下命令，事情也能行得通；自身行为不端正，即使三令五申，百姓也不会听从。"）

Confucius said, "If a ruler is upright, he could have things done without giving orders; if he is not, people would not listen to him even if he gives repeated orders." (*The Analects*)

zhī chǐ ér hòu yǒng 知耻而后勇

Having a Feeling of Shame Gives Rise to Courage.

知道耻辱之后就有了勇气。源于"知耻近乎勇"（知道耻辱就接近勇敢了）。"知耻"就是有羞恶之心（对自己的过错感到羞耻，对他人的不善感到憎恶），孟子（前372？—前289）将其视为人之为人的基准或底线之一。"勇"即勇气、勇敢。在儒家那里，它和"知"（智慧）、"仁"（仁爱）一起构成"三达德"（三种普世的德行）。将"知耻"和"勇"联系起来，意在激励人们要勇于面对自己的不足，奋发进取，为达到完美境界而努力。它是个人、企业、组织、民族、国家等自尊、自励、自强精神的体现。

The notion that having a feeling of shame gives rise to courage comes from the saying that "to have a feeling of shame is to be near to having courage." Having a feeling of shame means to be ashamed of one's own mistakes as well as to hate the misbehavior of others. Mencius (372?-289 BC) believed this to be one of the basic things humans must do. In Confucian thought courage is one of three universal virtues along with wisdom and love for others. Linking shame and courage was meant to impel people to face their shortcomings squarely and work hard for improvement and perfection. The concept embodies the spirit of individuals, companies, organizations, ethnic groups, and the whole nation in achieving self-respect, self-motivation, and self-improvement.

引例 Citations：

◎知、仁、勇三者，天下之达德也。(《礼记·中庸》)
（智慧、仁爱、勇敢是天下共通普遍的德行。）

Wisdom, love for others, and courage, these three are the universal virtues of all under heaven. (*The Book of Rites*)

◎好学近乎知，力行近乎仁，知耻近乎勇。(《礼记·中庸》)
（喜爱学习就接近了智，尽力实行就接近了仁，知道耻辱就接近了勇。）

To love learning is to be near to wisdom, to practice with vigor is to be near to love for others, and to have a feeling of shame is to be near to courage. (*The Book of Rites*)

zhīxíng-héyī 知行合一

Unity of Knowledge and Action

对"知""行"关系的一种认识。王阳明（1472—1529）基于心学

"心外无理"的主张，提出了"知行合一"说。他认为，对人伦日用之道的体认与践行不能割裂，二者是一体的两面。心中有所"知"必然会付诸行动，"行"是"知"的自然运用。若不"行"，便不是真正的"知"。另一方面，"行"也必然会带来深刻切实的认知。若没有"知"，仅仅是不自觉的或迫不得已的行为，便不能实现端正之"行"。

This is one interpretation of the relationship between "knowledge" and "action." Based on the concept in philosophy of the mind that "there are no li (理), or principles, outside the mind," Wang Yangming (1472-1529) made the argument that "there is unity of knowledge and action." He felt that it was impossible to separate an understanding of the principles underlying human relations in everyday life from the application of these principles, that these were two sides of the same thing. If there was "knowledge" in the mind, it would surely be put into practice, as "action" was the natural use of "knowledge." If it was not applied, it could not be true "knowledge." On the other hand, "action" would also bring about deeper knowledge. Without "knowledge," mere unconscious or forced behavior would not constitute proper "action."

引例 Citations：

◎外心以求理，此知行之所以二也；求理于吾心，此圣门知行合一之教。（《传习录》卷中）

（在心外寻求理，这是将知行分别为两件事的原因；在心中寻求理，这是圣门"知行合一"的教法。）

Searching for principles outside the mind is the reason why people separate knowledge from action; searching for principles within one's mind is how sages teach about the unity of knowledge and action. (*Records of Great Learning*)

◎知之真切笃实处，即是行；行之明觉精察处，即是知。知行工夫本不可离，只为后世学者分作两截用功，失却知行本体，故有合一并进之说。(《传习录》卷中)
(认知达到真切笃实的境地，便是"行"；践行达到明确的自觉和精微的省察，便是"知"。"知"与"行"的工夫原本不能割裂，只是因为后世的学者将二者作为两件事分别去用功，背离了"知""行"本来的状态，因此有知行合一并进之说。)

When knowledge is genuine and substantive, it becomes action; when actions bring about self-awareness and keen perceptions, they become knowledge. "Knowledge" and "action" were indivisible to begin with, and it was only because scholars later treated them as two separate things, contrary to their original nature, that there was a theory of their being united and developing together. (*Records of Great Learning*)

zhīxiān-xínghòu 知先行后

First Knowledge, Then Action

对"知""行"关系的一种认识。程颐（1033—1107）、朱熹（1130—1200）等人在"知""行"关系问题上主张"知先行后"。他们并不否认，对人伦日用之道的体认与践行是相互关联的，二者不可偏废。但若就先后而言，应以"知"为先。"知"是"行"的基础，"行"是在"知"的指导下实现的。只有先认识了人伦日用之道，才能使自己的言行符合道的要求。

The term represents one interpretation of the relationship between "knowledge" and "action." Regarding the relationship between "knowledge" and "action," scholars like Cheng Yi (1033-1107) and Zhu Xi (1130-1200) argued that "knowledge precedes action." They did not deny that an understanding of the principles underlying human relations in everyday life is interrelated with the application of these principles, nor did they feel that either of the two should be overlooked. However, in terms of sequence, they argued that "knowledge" came first, that it was the basis of "action," and that "action" took place through the guidance of "knowledge." Only by first understanding the principles underlying human relations in everyday life can we make our words and deeds follow the rules which govern human activities.

引例 Citations：

◎须是识在所行之先，譬如行路须得光照。(《二程遗书》卷三)

(必须是认识在行动之前，如同行路必须有光亮照明。)

Knowledge must be present before it can be acted upon, just as light must illuminate the path to be followed. (*Writings of the Cheng Brothers*)

◎知行常相须，如目无足不行，足无目不见。论先后，知为先；论轻重，行为重。(《朱子语类》卷九)

(知与行始终是相互依存的，如同眼睛没有足的功用不能前行，足没有眼睛的功用则不能视路。若说二者先后，知在行先；若说二者轻重，行更重要。)

Knowledge and action are interdependent, just as eyes cannot walk without the feet, and feet cannot see without the eyes. In terms of sequence, knowledge comes first; in terms of importance, action is more important. (*Categorized Conversations of Master Zhu Xi*)

zhí 直

Rectitude

"直"的基本含义是正直。具体而言，人们对"直"有两种不同的理解：其一，言行符合道德或礼法的要求，不因贪图个人的私利而行背德违法之事，即是"直"。不过由于人们对德礼的理解不同，对"直"的具体表现的认识也有所差异，甚至存在矛盾。其二，依据实情行事，不为迎合他人的期待或需求而隐瞒实情，也是"直"。

The basic meaning of "rectitude" is uprightness. More specifically, there are two interpretations of "rectitude." The first interpretation refers to words and deeds that meet the moral standards or the rules of propriety. To be "upright" is to refrain from doing anything immoral or illegal for the sake of personal gain. However, because there are different understandings of morality and propriety, there are also different views, even conflicting ones, of how "rectitude" is manifested. The second interpretation of being "upright" is acting in accordance with facts and not concealing the truth in order to meet the expectations or needs of others.

引例 Citations：

◎子曰："孰谓微生高直？或乞醯（xī）焉，乞诸其邻而与之。"（《论语·公冶长》）

（孔子言："谁说微生高正直？有人向他求取醋，他[不说自己没有，而]从邻居那里要来醋给他。"）

Confucius asked, "Who said Weisheng Gao is upright? Someone asked him for vinegar, and (without saying he did not have any) he got some from his neighbor for the man." (*The Analects*)

◎哀公问曰:"何为则民服?"孔子对曰:"举直错诸枉,则民服;举枉错诸直,则民不服。"(《论语•为政》)

(鲁哀公问道:"怎么做才能让百姓信服呢?"孔子答道:"将正直的人提拔起来放在邪曲的人之上,百姓就会信服;若是将邪曲的人提拔起来放在正直的人之上,百姓就不会信服。")

Duke Ai of the State of Lu asked, "How can I win over the people?" Confucius replied, "If you promote upright people and put them above crooked ones, you will win over the people; if you promote crooked people and put them above upright ones, you will not win over the people." (*The Analects*)

zhì dà guó ruò pēng xiǎo xiān 治大国若烹小鲜

Governing a Big Country Is Like Cooking Small Fish.

治理大国就像烹制小鱼一样。"小鲜"即小鱼。这是老子基于"无为"理念阐发的治理大国的基本原则。烹制小鱼,必须注意调和好各种佐料,精心掌握好火候,使每条小鱼都入味;同时不能多加搅动,多搅则易烂。与此相类,大国幅员辽阔,人口众多,各地域、阶层的差别大,治国者要精心周到,统筹兼顾,使政策措施惠及每一个人;国家大政方针一旦确立,施政者不要过多干预社会生活。

Governing a big country is like cooking small fish. This is a fundamental principle of state governance based on the concept of "non-action" advocated by Laozi. When cooking small fish, one needs to mix various kinds of ingredients, carefully control time of cooking and degree of heating, so that every small fish is equally tasty. One should not stir the fish too much in cooking so that they will not fall apart into small pieces. Similarly, as a big country has a vast territory, a large population, and wide differences among regions and social groups, those who govern the land must be meticulous and thoughtful and take all factors into consideration, so that their policies and measures benefit everyone. Once fundamental policies for governance are adopted, those who govern should not intervene excessively in social activities.

引例 Citation：

◎治大国，若烹小鲜。以道莅天下，其鬼不神；非其鬼不神，其神不伤人；非其神不伤人，圣人亦不伤人。夫两不相伤，故德交归焉。(《老子·六十章》)

(治理大国，就像煎烹小鱼。用"道"治理天下，鬼神起不了作用；不仅鬼神不起作用，而且鬼神的作用伤不了人；不但鬼神的作用伤害不了人，圣人有道也不会伤害人。这样，鬼神和圣人都不伤害人，所以所有的德惠都归于民众。)

Governing a big country is like cooking small fish. When the country is ruled by Dao, demons can neither disrupt it nor harm the people. Even sages acting in Dao principles will not bring harm to people either. Free from harms by demons and sages, people stand to gain all benefits. (*Laozi*)

zhōng 忠

Loyalty

"忠"是一种尽己所能的态度。处在某一身份或职位的人应全心全意地履行其职责,而不应受个人私利的影响。"忠"的对象可以是赋予其职分的个人,也可以是其履职的组织、团体乃至国家。例如在古代社会,人们认为君主应该忠于民众,臣属应该忠于君主。

Loyalty involves doing one's utmost. A person in a certain position or office should wholeheartedly perform his duties and must not be influenced by personal interests. The object of loyalty can be the person who appoints you to your post or grants you a position; it can also be an organization, group or the state where you belong. For example, in ancient society it was thought the monarch should be loyal to the people while the subjects should be loyal to the monarch.

引例 Citations：

◎曾子曰："吾日三省吾身：为人谋而不忠乎？与朋友交而不信乎？传不习乎？"(《论语·学而》)

(曾子言："我每日多次反省自己：为他人谋划是否未尽忠心？与朋友交往是否不守信诺？传授的学问是否没有温习？")

Zengzi said, "Each day I reflect on myself several times. Have I failed to be loyal to someone when offering my advice to him? Have I failed to keep my word to my friends? Have I failed to review the teachings I have learned?" (*The Analects*)

◎尽己之谓忠。(朱熹《论语集注》卷一)

(竭尽自己所能就是忠。)

To do all one can is what loyalty requires. (Zhu Xi: *The Analects Variorum*)

术语表 List of Concepts

英文	中文
A Benevolent Person Loves Others.	仁者爱人
A Broad Mind Achieves Greatness.	有容乃大
A Just Cause Enjoys Abundant Support While an Unjust Cause Finds Little.	得道多助，失道寡助
All the People Within the Four Seas Are Brothers.	四海之内皆兄弟
Arrive at the Same Destination via Different Routes / Rely on a Common Ontological Entity	同归殊途
Be Sincere in Thought	诚意
Being both Opposite and Complementary	相反相成
Being Considerate / Forgiveness	恕
Broad-mindedness / Unconstrained Style	旷达
Careful Reflection and Clear Discrimination	慎思明辨
Carry or Overturn the Boat / Make or Break	载舟覆舟
Change	变化
Character Endowed by Heaven	天命之性
Character Endowed by *Qi* (Vital Force)	气质之性
Ci (Lyric)	词
Ci (Lyric) and *Qu* (Melody)	词曲
Classical Elegance	典雅
Combine Toughness with Softness	刚柔相济
Ding (Vessel)	鼎

英文	中文
Do Away with the Old and Set Up the New	革故鼎新
Entrust One's Thoughts and Feelings to Imagery	寄托
Ethereal Effect	空灵
Exert One's Heart / Mind to the Utmost	尽心
Exquisite Skill Looks Simple and Clumsy.	大巧若拙
Fairness Fosters Discernment and Integrity Creates Authority.	公生明，廉生威
Fenggu	风骨
Fiction	小说
Fine Music	雅乐
First Action, Then Knowledge	行先知后
First Knowledge, Then Action	知先行后
Freehand Brushwork	写意
Gilded and Colored	错彩镂金
Governance Means Rectitude.	政者正也
Governing a Big Country Is Like Cooking Small Fish.	治大国若烹小鲜
Great Truth in Simple Words	大道至简
Having a Feeling of Shame Gives Rise to Courage.	知耻而后勇
He Who Repeatedly Commits Wrongdoing Will Come to No Good End.	多行不义必自毙
Hold Actualities According to Its Name	循名责实
Indifference to Fame and Fortune Characterizes a High Aim in Life, and Leading a Quiet Life Helps One Accomplish Something Lasting.	淡泊明志，宁静致远
Inner Beauty	内美

英文	中文
Knowledge from One's Moral Nature	德性之知
Knowledge from One's Senses	见闻之知
Lotus Rising Out of Water	芙蓉出水
Loyalty	忠
Make a Fresh Start with the People	与民更始
Mandate of Heaven	天命
Maximal Functioning	大用
Melancholy	沉郁
Mind Cognition	心知
Moral Cultivation	风教
Movement and Stillness	动静
Natural Grace	飘逸
Natural Law / Principles of Heaven	天理
Noble Spirit	浩然之气
One Thing in Two Fundamental States	一物两体
Overly Elaborative	繁缛
Painting in Colors	丹青
Past Experience, If Not Forgotten, Is a Guide for the Future.	前事不忘，后事之师
People with No Covetous Desires Stand Upright.	无欲则刚
Plain Line Drawing	白描
Professionalism	当行
Qi (Vessel)	器

英文	中文
Qigu (Emotional Vitality and Forcefulness)	气骨
Qu (Melody)	曲
Quiet Living with No Worldly Desire	淡泊
Reciprocity as a Social Norm	礼尚往来
Rectification of Names	正名
Rectify One's Heart / Mind	正心
Rectitude	直
Repay a Grudge with Rectitude	以直报怨
Review the Old and Learn the New	温故知新
Review the Past to Understand the Present	鉴古知今
Search for the Lost Heart	求放心
See Things as Equal	齐物
Shendu (Ethical Self-cultivation)	慎独
Shi (Poetry)	诗
Song	歌
Support All People by Upholding Truth and Justice	道济天下
Survival of a Nation Is the Responsibility of Every Individual.	天下兴亡，匹夫有责
Taixu (Great Void)	太虚
Teaching How to Fish	授人以渔
The Fiery Emperor and the Yellow Emperor / Emperor Yan and Emperor Huang	炎黄
The Major Organ and the Minor Organs	大体 / 小体

英文	中文
The Spring and Autumn Annals / The Spring and Autumn Period	春秋
There Is But One *Li* (Universal Principle), Which Exists in Diverse Forms.	理一分殊
Think Carefully Before Taking Action	三思而行
Think of Righteousness in the Face of Gain	见利思义
Three Elements	三才
Three Standards	三表
Troops Will Be Powerful When Fighting a Just Cause.	师直为壮
Unity of Knowledge and Action	知行合一
Vitality / Vital Force	血气
Way of Heaven	天道
When Seeing a Person of High Caliber, Strive to Be His Equal.	见贤思齐
When Worse Comes to the Worst, Things Will Turn for the Better.	否极泰来
Words Can Fully Express Thought.	言尽意
Words Cannot Fully Express Thought.	言不尽意
Wu Is the Origin.	以无为本
Xiang (Semblance)	象
Xuan (Mystery)	玄

中国历史年代简表 A Brief Chronology of Chinese History

夏 Xia Dynasty		2070-1600 BC
商 Shang Dynasty		1600-1046 BC
周 Zhou Dynasty		1046-256 BC
周 Zhou Dynasty	西周 Western Zhou Dynasty	1046-771 BC
	东周 Eastern Zhou Dynasty	770-256 BC
秦 Qin Dynasty		221-206 BC
汉 Han Dynasty		206 BC-AD 220
汉 Han Dynasty	西汉 Western Han Dynasty	206 BC-AD 25
	东汉 Eastern Han Dynasty	25-220
三国 Three Kingdoms		220-280
三国 Three Kingdoms	魏 Kingdom of Wei	220-265
	蜀 Kingdom of Shu	221-263
	吴 Kingdom of Wu	222-280
晋 Jin Dynasty		265-420
晋 Jin Dynasty	西晋 Western Jin Dynasty	265-317
	东晋 Eastern Jin Dynasty	317-420
南北朝 Southern and Northern Dynasties		420-589
南北朝 Southern and Northern Dynasties	南朝 Southern Dynasties	420-589
	南朝 Southern Dynasties 宋 Song Dynasty	420-479
	齐 Qi Dynasty	479-502
	梁 Liang Dynasty	502-557
	陈 Chen Dynasty	557-589

南北朝 Southern and Northern Dynasties	北朝 Northern Dynasties	北朝 Northern Dynasties	386-581
		北魏 Northern Wei Dynasty	386-534
		东魏 Eastern Wei Dynasty	534-550
		北齐 Northern Qi Dynasty	550-577
		西魏 Western Wei Dynasty	535-556
		北周 Northern Zhou Dynasty	557-581
隋 Sui Dynasty			581-618
唐 Tang Dynasty			618-907
五代 Five Dynasties			907-960
五代 Five Dynasties	后梁 Later Liang Dynasty		907-923
	后唐 Later Tang Dynasty		923-936
	后晋 Later Jin Dynasty		936-947
	后汉 Later Han Dynasty		947-950
	后周 Later Zhou Dynasty		951-960
宋 Song Dynasty			960-1279
宋 Song Dynasty	北宋 Northern Song Dynasty		960-1127
	南宋 Southern Song Dynasty		1127-1279
辽 Liao Dynasty			907-1125
西夏 Western Xia Dynasty			1038-1227
金 Jin Dynasty			1115-1234
元 Yuan Dynasty			1206-1368
明 Ming Dynasty			1368-1644
清 Qing Dynasty			1616-1911
中华民国 Republic of China			1912-1949
中华人民共和国 People's Republic of China			Founded on October 1, 1949